IN
TOO
DEEP

Since 1996, Bloomberg Press has published books for financial professionals, as well as books of general interest in investing, economics, current affairs, and policy affecting investors and business people. Titles are written by well-known practitioners, BLOOMBERG NEWS® reporters and columnists, and other leading authorities and journalists. Bloomberg Press books have been translated into more than 20 languages.

For a list of available titles, please visit out Web site at www.wiley.com/go/bloombergpress.

IN
TOO
DEEP

BP AND THE DRILLING RACE
THAT TOOK IT DOWN

STANLEY REED
ALISON FITZGERALD

BLOOMBERG PRESS
An Imprint of
WILEY

Published by John Wiley & Sons, Inc., Hoboken, New Jersey.
Published simultaneously in Canada.

For general information on our other products and services or for technical support, please
contact our Customer Care Department within the United States at (800) 762-2974,
outside the United States at (317) 572-3993 or fax (317) 572-4002.

Wiley also publishes its books in a variety of electronic formats. Some content that appears
in print may not be available in electronic books. For more information about Wiley
products, visit our web site at www.wiley.com.

Library of Congress Cataloging-in-Publication Data:
Reed, Stanley, 1950–
    In too deep : BP and the drilling race that took it down / Stanley Reed, Alison
Fitzgerald.
        p.   cm.—(Bloomberg ; 137)
    Includes index.
    ISBN 978-0-470-95090-6 (hardback); ISBN 978-1-118-02319-8 (ebk.);
ISBN 978-1-118-02320-4 (ebk.); ISBN 978-1-118-02321-1 (ebk.)
    1. BP Deepwater Horizon Explosion and Oil Spill, 2010.   2. Oil wells—
Mexico, Gulf of—Blowouts.   3. BP (Firm)   I. Fitzgerald, Alison.   II. Title.
TD427.P4R39   2011
363.738'20916364—dc22

                                                                        2010045651

Printed in the United States of America
10 9 8 7 6 5 4 3 2 1

For Katherine, Katy, and Matt.
— SR

For Drew, with tons of love,
and Nikita, Elijah, and Forrest,
the greatest kids on earth.
—AF

For the thing which I greatly feared is come upon me, and that which I was afraid of is come unto me.

I was not in safety, neither had I rest, neither was I quiet; yet trouble came.

Job 3:25–26

Contents

Cast of Characters

BP Executives

John Browne	CEO, 1995–2007
Tony Hayward	CEO, 2007–2010
Robert Dudley	CEO, October 1, 2010–present
Andy Inglis	Head of BP Exploration and Production, 2007–2010
David I. Rainey	Vice President, Gulf of Mexico Exploration
Cindy A. Yeilding	Exploration Manager, Gulf of Mexico Exploration

Deepwater Horizon Workers

Michael Williams	Chief Electronics Technician for Transocean Ltd.
Stephen Bertone	Chief Engineer for Transocean Ltd.
Doug Brown	Chief Mechanic for Transocean Ltd.
Jimmy Harrell	Offshore Installation Manager, Transocean Ltd.
Donald Vidrine	Well Site Leader, BP PLC
Robert Kaluza	Well Site Leader, BP PLC

Washington, D.C.

Barack Obama	President of the United States
Congressman Bart Stupak	Chairman of the Subcommittee on Oversight and Investigations, House Energy and Commerce Committee
Congressman Henry Waxman	Chairman of the House Energy and Commerce Committee

Others

Mikhail M. Fridman	One of Russia's richest men, chairman of Alfa Group and TNK-BP
Brent Coon	Plaintiff's lawyer in Beaumont, Texas, who led the lawsuits against BP after the company's Texas City refinery exploded
Dave Senko	Construction Manager, J.E. Merit Constructors, a subsidiary of Jacobs Engineering Group Inc.

Authors' Note

Both of us will likely remember 2010 as our BP and Gulf of Mexico year. We spent months reporting on and writing about the aftermath of the April 20 explosion and subsequent oil spill. Alison Fitzgerald tracked down survivors and relatives of the victims and attended many of the hearings trying to understand what caused the fatal accident. She dug through documents, read transcripts, and spent time with lawyers and investigators who were already familiar with BP. Bloomberg dispatched Stanley Reed from London to rural Louisiana to try to make contact with BP's senior executives. He wound up having dinner with CEO Tony Hayward in a restaurant in Houma, where BP was coordinating its cleanup effort.

The two of us came to the story from very different perspectives. Reed, a Middle East and oil specialist, had been covering BP and other oil companies for more than a decade, mostly as the London bureau chief of *BusinessWeek* magazine. Over the years he had spent hours with BP's influential CEO, John Browne, traveling with him to Russia and dining at his home. He also knew Browne's successor,

Tony Hayward, well and had even spent time with the man who was to be Hayward's heir, Robert Dudley. He had been out to BP's pride and joy in the Gulf, the Thunder Horse platform, less than a year before. He had spent a day in Houston with BP's Gulf explorers, hearing them explain how they found oil in what they said was the trickiest patch of geology in the world. Fitzgerald, a Washington-based investigative reporter, hadn't had as much contact with the oil industry. She was assigned to the story so that she could bring to bear her sleuthing skills, vast range of Washington contacts, and knowledge of the regulatory and political spheres.

We were drawn to the story by shock and sorrow over the violent deaths of the Deepwater Horizon rig workers, as well as dismay over the extraordinary tide of pollution that spewed from the stricken well. We wanted to know why this tragic incident had occurred under the watch of BP and not another company such as ExxonMobil.

We found that there was in fact a reason.

The story behind the Macondo blowout is more than a story about technical failures or human error. The root cause, we found, may lie in BP's particular corporate culture, which depends on and even celebrates calculated risk taking. The company's corporate DNA is different from its competitors, where engineering principles dominate. BP is more of a financial culture. BP is very creative at finding oil and persuading governments to open their doors. But it is sometimes less good at everyday operations.

The Deepwater Horizon disaster was not the company's first large-scale industrial accident. Five years before, 15 workers had died in a massive explosion at a BP refinery called Texas City just outside of Houston. There were other close calls as well.

Today's BP was created by the combination of several major oil companies that were packaged together in a merger spree by Lord Browne. Browne pushed the stodgy BP to be a growth company and became one of the most admired CEOs of his time. He saw that there was big money to be made by putting companies together, wringing out costs, and investing in their best prospects. He took advantage of a rare moment in history when nations long off-limits to western companies suddenly opened their doors. The question is whether he went too fast and failed to pay close enough attention to integrating the merged companies and ensuring that their operations—pipelines, refineries, and production platforms—were up to standards. Hayward himself said near the end of Browne's tenure that BP needed to slow down.

Browne also may not have foreseen all the consequences of his drive to improve financial performance. When put under pressure, people sometimes make poor choices that compromise safety. From the information that has emerged so far, that is what happened in the blowout. People in a hurry made bad decisions. They convinced themselves that a dangerously defective well was safe.

The oil industry is inherently dangerous because it works with volatile substances under pressure. Companies need to be constantly vigilant to prevent accidents. Slipups kill people, sometimes many people. Tragically, that is what happened both at Texas City and on the Deepwater Horizon.

In closing, we would like to remember those who died:

Deepwater Horizon, April 20, 2010
Jason Anderson
Aaron Dale Burkeen
Donald Clark
Stephen Curtis
Gordon Jones
Roy Wyatt Kemp
Karl Kleppinger
Blair Manuel
Dewey Revette
Shane Roshto
Adam Weise

Texas City Refinery, March 23, 2005

Glenn Bolton

Lorena Cruz-Alexander

Rafael "Ralph" Herrera Jr.

Daniel J. Hogan III

Jimmy Ray Hunnings

Morris "Monk" King

Larry Wayne Linsenbardt

Arthur Galvan Ramos

Ryan Rodriguez

James Warren Rowe

Linda Marie Hammer Rowe

Kimberly Smith

Susan Duhan Taylor

Larry Sheldon Thomas

Eugene White

Prologue

July 27, 2010, was a fine day for a corporate execution in London. Television vans filled the parking bays across from a quiet, fenced park with high trees, located outside the British Petroleum Public Liability Company's (BP PLC) tan, brick headquarters. The cameras were there to see the giant oil company's CEO, Tony Hayward, take the fall for the Gulf of Mexico disaster that had killed 11 men, spilled an estimated 4.9 million barrels of oil, and made the company a pariah in the United States—its most important market. Indeed, what had occurred under Hayward had jeopardized the future of the entire oil industry in the Gulf and brought BP itself close to the abyss.

A handful of reporters, many of whom had covered BP for years, were invited inside. Soon, three men joined them in a meeting room sparsely furnished with wooden chairs and a handsome wooden table created by the Queen's grandson, Viscount Linley, whose expensive, handmade furniture was admired by Hayward's predecessor, John Browne. Hayward made the rounds, shaking hands. Then he and his newly appointed successor, Robert Dudley, flanked the company's tall, elegantly-dressed Swedish Chairman, Carl-Henric Svanberg, who announced that, by mutual agreement with the board, "Tony is stepping down and Bob is taking over." Svanberg said he was sad.

Hayward's swaggering, gaffe-plagued effort to lead BP's response to the spill had made him a figure of scorn and ridicule in the United States. The *New Yorker* magazine even satirized him as "Chef Tony," author of a cookbook with oily dishes such as "blackened prawns" and "thick-as-tar chocolate pudding." Just months before, he was in command of one of the world's largest and most profitable companies. BP was the Goldman Sachs of the oil industry, as one veteran executive said: cutting edge and always on top. In what had been a slow-to-change industry, it was a company that was innovative and on-the-move, playing on the political and technological frontiers.

As CEO, Hayward had been like a chief of state, roving the world on a corporate jet, feted everywhere BP had operations, from the royal palaces of the Gulf sheikdoms to the Kremlin. Now, just three years into his job, he was being made to walk the plank, thanks to some disastrous misjudgments by people drilling what should have been a relatively simple oil well. Up until early July, Hayward had some hope of surviving in his job, but activist board members thought his staying on would be toxic to BP's future. Many people inside BP thought the company and Hayward were victims of bad luck because the accident could have happened to anyone. But in an industry that claims all accidents are preventable, this one hadn't been prevented. In fact, many industry insiders say it happened to BP for a reason, and that it was years in the making. After a string of industrial accidents and close calls, BP executives, including Hayward, hadn't learned the lessons that presented themselves from repeated investigations. The board, one BP official said, was determined that there would be no reward for failure.

This book presents the story of BP's meteoric rise and then Hayward's and the company's sudden fall. The tumble was especially shocking because Hayward had tried to banish the mishaps that wrecked the last years of his predecessor, John Browne. Lord Browne was the CEO whose mega-deals and outspokenness on climate change had raised BP's public profile. But like Browne, whose tenure ended badly in 2007, Hayward wound up being fodder for the television cameras and photographers waiting to record his downfall. Being CEO of what many consider Britain's most important company has its drawbacks as well as benefits.

Asked if he thought he had been unfairly judged—after all, he had been tossed out even before BP published its own investigation of the incident—Hayward sounded almost Shakespearean. He said, "I think, frankly, what is fair or unfair is not the point. The fact is that I did lead the response and, as a consequence, I became the public face of BP; and as a consequence of that I was demonized and vilified. And the fact is that BP cannot move on as a company in the United States with me as its leader. It is not possible, and that is the reality."

Dudley, Hayward's successor, who grew up in Mississippi and has a more natural affinity for the Gulf, faces a future full of unknowns, especially in the United States, the company's most important center of operations. "It is not our intention to exit the U.S.," he said, "Nor do we believe we will not be able to operate there." But what proposition BP now has to offer governments that control access to resources, investors, and, indeed, its own employees is in question. As Amy Myers Jaffe of the James A. Baker III Institute for Public Policy at Rice University put it: "If you were a politician, would you want to be responsible for giving BP a lease?"

Chapter 1

Night of Horror, Day of Triumph

M ike Williams just finished a day of routine maintenance on the offshore drilling rig Deepwater Horizon. Short on sleep, because today was the day he was rotating from the night to day shifts, Williams was testing and repairing electrical equipment, then filled in some overdue paperwork. By 9:30 that night, he was in his electronics shop, talking to his wife on the phone. Williams was the chief electronics engineer on the rig, which was in the middle of the Gulf of Mexico drilling a well for the oil giant BP PLC. He'd been away for about 10 days and had another 10 to go before he'd be heading home.

Through the phone Williams' wife heard someone over a loudspeaker announce that gas levels on the Horizon were high. "Do you need to go take care of that?" she asked her husband. He downplayed the importance of the warning. "We'd gotten them so frequently that I'd become immune to them," Mike Williams said afterward. "I didn't even hear them anymore, especially with this well. With this well, we were getting gas back all the time."

Just a few months before the Horizon had triumphantly completed the deepest well in history, in a BP discovery called the Tiber field. The Horizon then moved to this spot, about 42 miles off the coast of Louisiana, to drill in a part of the Gulf called Mississippi Canyon. The well was called Macondo, after the fictional "city of mirrors" in Colombian author Gabriel Garcia Marquez' masterpiece *One Hundred Years of Solitude*. The city, in the end, is destroyed by a hurricane. The Transocean Inc. rig and crew, hired by BP, had hit oil at Macondo weeks before and had spent April 20th preparing to plug the well with cement in order to move on to the next hole. BP would come back later to tie Macondo up to an oil production platform that would harvest the crude. BP press officers were preparing a press release announcing the find.

Williams soon heard a loud hissing noise and became concerned. He told his wife it was time to hang up and find out what was going on. He assumed the hiss was some sort of hydraulic leak, nothing particularly dangerous.

Doug Brown, the chief mechanic working in the engine control room next door, heard it too. Over in the living quarters, Stephen Bertone had just finished a shower, and was lying on his bed, about to begin reading a book, when the hissing began. It grew louder and louder until it sounded like a freight train storming through his room. The hiss was soon followed by a cacophony of alarms. Then a voice over the P.A. system warned a nearby service ship to back away from the Horizon because the rig was in a "well control situation," a mundane-sounding term that really means disaster could be moments away.

As Williams pushed back from his desk to find out what was wrong, the entire rig began to shake. His computer monitor exploded, and all the lights in his room popped, leaving him—and everyone else on the rig—in the dark. He headed for the door as the hiss got louder and louder; he now realized the sound came from the ship's engines which were feeding on the natural gas that filled the air. "It was higher than I could possibly describe. It was spinning so fast," Williams said. Suddenly the spinning engines stopped and a huge explosion rocked the Deepwater Horizon, blowing the fire-safe door to Williams' shop off its hinges and directly into the electronics technician, knocking him back several feet against the back wall and to the floor.

The blast threw Brown against his control panels, and then down through a hole that opened on the floor. "I was wondering what was happening. I was confused. I was hurting. I was dazed, and I proceeded to try to get up and the second explosion happened." That blast threw him into the hole a second time, and the ceiling caved in upon him.

After the first explosion, Bertone put on his boots, life vest and hard hat and headed for the door; he could smell and taste fuel in the air. He knew it was an emergency and that he had a muster station to get to, and possibly a fire to battle. Then there was the second boom. The hallway was strewn with debris. He headed for the bridge.

Williams was crawling through the darkness toward the door of the electronics shop, gasping for breath as the CO_2 systems, designed to starve any fire of oxygen, also starved his own lungs. He held a penlight between his teeth, but it failed to cut through the smoke-filled darkness. He made it through his exploded doorframe, and headed to the next fire door. As he reached for that handle, the second blast blew the second door off its hinges, sending another wall of steel hurtling into his body. "The doors were beating me to death," Williams, a burly, goateed man with ruddy skin, said. "Two doors in a row hit me right in the forehead. My arm wouldn't work and my left leg wouldn't work, I couldn't breathe and I couldn't see."

Williams crawled, blind, across the bare grid where floor panels had once been. He crawled over the bodies of two men he couldn't identify, nor help. Brown, who had pulled himself out of the hole in the floor, was crawling beside Williams, both searching for a way out and air. They found the exit, found air to breathe, and turned to head upwind of the fire and smoke. Williams paused to wipe blood from his eyes, and found the walkway before him, the railing, and entire wall had been blown away in the explosion. The voice of Andrea Fleytas, the rig's dynamic positioning officer, was blaring over the PA system, calling "Mayday, Mayday."

Brown helped Williams along. "He was dazed, confused. He was screaming he had to get out of here, and he had a wound on his forehead and he was bleeding profusely," said Brown. The hissing had turned into a roar, and Williams could see that the doghouse, a storage and break room on the rig floor, and half the derrick, which rises 242 feet into the sky, were aflame. "At that moment, I realized there was a blowout," Williams said. He eyed an empty lifeboat in the distance and, in his terror, flirted with the notion of jumping in and launching it to save himself. Instead, he and Brown headed for the bridge, the emergency station they had rehearsed going to in so many drills. "I had responsibilities," Williams said.

Brown and Williams reached the bridge, which was in complete chaos. "They were trying to get systems going. They were trying to get control back," Brown said. There were no engines, no thrusters, no telephones—no power at all. When Bertone arrived on the bridge he heard someone yelling, "The engine room, ECR, and pump room are gone. They're all gone." The man was covered in blood and Bertone didn't recognize him.

"What do you mean, gone?" Bertone demanded.

"They've blown up. They're all gone. They've blown up."

It was then that Bertone recognized the voice of Michael Williams, who was also screaming at the captain, "We need to abandon ship now!" Bertone tried to staunch the bleeding from Williams' forehead with toilet paper. Captain Carl Kuchta told them to remain calm as he tried to figure out what to do about the lost power. The only way to save the rig would be to get the engines going again so they could fight the fire.

Bertone volunteered to head back toward the fire and try to start the backup generator, the only hope of saving the Horizon. Williams told him he could not go alone. He grabbed Bertone's shirt, and they headed through the door toward the blaze. The emergency generator was across the deck. The men tried repeatedly to start it up. They failed. When they returned to the bridge, Captain Kuchta determined the fire was out of control and ordered the remaining crewmembers to abandon ship.

Williams, Bertone, and Fleytas left the bridge only to find that both lifeboats at their end of the rig had already been launched. The fire blazed between them and the remaining two. The air was popping and sizzling, pieces of hot metal rained down on them, and the flames were starting to wrap around the rig in search of oxygen.

With no lifeboats, the crewmembers found the inflatable emergency rafts, and put an injured mate on a stretcher aboard the first. Bertone and several others climbed in with him and they were lowered into the water. The fire was so hot now that Williams decided there wasn't time to launch another raft. Fleytas, still on deck, was yelling, "We're going to die!"

"I honestly didn't believe that we would survive trying to deploy a life raft. I decided we can stay here and die or we can jump," Williams recalled.

He turned to Fleytas and told her it was time to run and jump. She said she couldn't possibly jump the 10 stories from the blazing rig to the dark waters below. "I said, 'Watch me then.' I took off running, and I jumped," Williams said. Fleytas followed.

By the following day, 11 crewmembers were dead and dozens more, including Williams, were injured. The Deepwater Horizon was ablaze in the middle of the Gulf, and would soon tip over and sink into the depths, leaving an open wellhead with oil gushing into the tropical waters.

The BP and Transocean drillers on the Deepwater Horizon were all working for one of the most powerful men in BP. Andy Inglis had been the right-hand man of CEO Tony Hayward since 2004. When Hayward got the top job, following the ouster of the legendary John Browne in 2007, Inglis took over the exploration and production (E&P) unit, an elite group at BP that accounted for most of the company's profits and that was used to getting its own way.

During the reign of Inglis, E&P's stature grew even more, and so did the importance of the Gulf of Mexico. He moved his unit's headquarters to Houston, away from the meddling bureaucrats in London. Even though it was located across the ocean, it was clear that E&P was the heart and soul of BP. The company's most recent annual report was emblazoned with the title: "Operating at the Energy Frontiers."

In the three years since Hayward took the top job at BP, Inglis had been used to reporting a string of successes to his boss. Now, early in the morning of April 21, he had a very different job. He rang Hayward, who was in the habit of staying at the Haymarket Hotel, a cozy London establishment near BP's offices, on weekdays. Hayward was eating breakfast when Inglis told him there was a blowout in the Gulf and people were missing. Hayward says his first reaction was "unprintable." What he thought he had worked hard to prevent had happened—and his best business unit was responsible.

Only nine months earlier Inglis was at the top of his game. On a steamy July day in 2009, he held court in the cabin of a wood-paneled corporate jet as it took off into the early morning skies from Sugarland Regional Airport, in the Houston suburbs. Inglis was accustomed to having private jets at his disposal. He spent much of his work life visiting BP's far flung empire, and oil chiefs rarely fly commercial. Today, he was taking a guest to BP's showcase development in the Gulf of Mexico, a massive oil production platform called Thunder Horse.

On the short hop to Houma, Louisiana, BP's base for ferrying people and supplies to its growing number of installations in the Gulf of Mexico, Inglis—pronounced "Ingalls"—unfolded a table, flipped through a bound set of charts and graphics, and gave a simple presentation, a kind of BP 101. The one thing that is crucial for a company like BP is finding new oil and gas to replace what you remove. If you fail in that task, you are eventually out of business—you are dead. Many companies struggle to replace their output; BP does not, Inglis said. It has been consistently adding more oil to its reserves than it produces, he said. In 2009, the company said it had found more oil than it pumped from the ground for 17 straight years. Inglis gave much of the credit for this performance to a strategy first laid out by former CEO John Browne in the early 1990s. As Inglis explained, BP doesn't waste its energy on small-potatoes projects. Instead, it focuses on finding and being the first to exploit giant fields of a billion barrels or more because these bring the scale and follow-on opportunities that can keep a company in business for a long time and earn it big money.

OIL SLEUTH

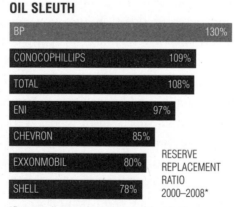

BP	130%
CONOCOPHILLIPS	109%
TOTAL	108%
ENI	97%
CHEVRON	85%
EXXONMOBIL	80%
SHELL	78%

RESERVE REPLACEMENT RATIO 2000–2008*

*Reserves discovered as percentage of production, excluding asset purchases and sales.

BP's oil explorers have better success than their competitors in finding new oil to replace the oil that the company produces from its existing wells. This ensures BP has plenty of oil to produce and sell in the future.

Source: Stanley Reed, "BP Rolls the Dice," *BusinessWeek*, September 14, 2009, p. 48. Data: Exane BNP Paribas.

The strategy means working on the frontier, a word that in the oil business has more than one meaning. Sometimes the frontier is an edgy political regime such as in Russia or Iraq, where BP has taken risks to gain a step on its peers. Sometimes it's the boundaries of technology, such as drilling and producing oil in water a mile deep or more. BP has taken the lead in deepwater zones, including the Gulf of Mexico and off Angola. The national oil companies that control much of the world's remaining oil reserves need multinational behemoths such as BP to develop such challenging resources. They don't need them to develop or maintain plain vanilla oil fields, and in those situations they are tempted to squeeze their foreign partners or throw them out entirely. That's why BP, Inglis said, was not interested in low margin, low risk work. "We don't do simple things," Inglis said. "We are prepared to work on the frontier and to manage the risks."

Inglis, a chunky teddy bear of a man with a full head of wavy hair and bright eyes is, by all accounts, reticent, especially with strangers. But when he warms to a subject, he looks you straight in the eye and talks with great enthusiasm in his north of England accent. That was how he was behaving on this day, and why not? Since Hayward became CEO in 2007, making Ingalls the top man in E&P, the pair had done much to right the faltering company after the messy exit of their mentor, the legendary Browne. The multibillion-dollar Thunder Horse platform, for example, had been plagued by years of delays and had even been left listing to one side in 2005 by hurricane Dennis, nearly sinking. Now the giant platform and the two oil fields it drained, Thunder Horse North and South, were performing superbly, producing 250,000 barrels per day of some of BP's most profitable oil and another 50,000 barrels or so of natural gas. Some of the eight existing wells feeding the platform—there would eventually be around 25—were producing a company-best 55,000 barrels per day for BP and its archrival ExxonMobil, which was BP's 25 percent junior partner in Thunder Horse.

Turning things around at Thunder Horse wasn't Inglis's only recent accomplishment. At the end of June 2009, in Baghdad, BP had rolled the dice and snatched the crown jewel of Iraq away from ExxonMobil, the magnificent, if decrepit, Rumaila oil field. BP won what was called a technical service contract with a lowball bid that would bring the company just $2 for each incremental barrel of oil it managed to squeeze out. BP bet it could do so at very low cost. By comparison, the company may make $20 or more on a Gulf of Mexico barrel. BP and its partner, China National Petroleum Corp., agreed to what might be the most ambitious expansion of an oil field of all time: taking the Iraqi field from its present one million barrels per day to almost 3 million barrels at an estimated cost of $20 billion. That feat would make Rumaila the world's most productive field outside of Saudi Arabia.

So daring was the gambit for what could be one of the world's great oil fields that, according to BP's head of exploration, Michael Daly, the Iraq team spent the ensuing weekend agonizing over whether the move was a stroke of genius or a blunder. They hoped their deal would put them in pole position for other Iraq ventures that came up, but they knew that they had only allowed themselves a slim margin, while exposing BP to huge political and security risks. They only began to feel more comfortable when other companies including ExxonMobil later followed suit, offering similarly low fees on lesser Iraqi fields.

Rumaila wasn't a new field. It had actually been discovered by BP in the 1950s. But it had been off limits to international companies for decades, was badly neglected, and represented a potentially huge opportunity because of the tens of billions of barrels of oil that remained underground there. Inglis argued that the project was worthwhile because it would give BP access to large quantities of oil for a very long time. "Long flat barrels" was how he described Rumaila's future contribution to BP's portfolio. More important, it would give

BP an early advantage in what could, along with Saudi Arabia and Russia, be one of the three most important oil- and gas-producing countries in the world. At the time, word around the company was that executives figured that if it went well—a big if—their returns could be in the mid-teens.

● ● ●

After the obligatory safety briefing at the airstrip, the big helicopter taking the BP party lifted gently off the runway and flew over the bayous and out into the Gulf of Mexico, dodging thunderstorms that looked like gray curtains coming down to the edge of the waves. A kind of oil field history unfolded below as rickety platforms close to shore gave way to more and more sophisticated installations farther out. Finally, after about an hour and a half, Thunder Horse, with its giant red pontoons, came into view.

BP executives liked to bring visitors to Thunder Horse to show off the company's technological prowess and, frankly, its guts. One hundred and fifty miles southeast of New Orleans, this gigantic platform, the size of a sports stadium, was as good a symbol as any of BP's leadership in a region that is the heart of the American oil industry. Thunder Horse floats in 6,000 feet of water, tethered by huge chains that can move the platform around so as to position it for drilling new wells. A two-decades long, multibillion-dollar campaign had paid off for BP in the Gulf of Mexico. In June 2008, Thunder Horse began producing oil, starting with a single well and rapidly building toward its over 300,000 barrel per day plateau. Other big deepwater projects with names like Mad Dog and Atlantis have also come on line in recent years. BP had the most production in the Gulf of any oil company, the most leases for drilling, and what looked like the best future. Part of that future lay beneath the blue waters to the West, where Inglis knew there was a trove of oil even more promising than Thunder Horse.

But Thunder Horse was the bird in the hand now. A Cambridge-educated mechanical engineer, Inglis revels in the intricacies of the equipment and likes to get his hands dirty. Thunder Horse was a special treat for him since many of the components had to be custom-designed. This was because of the presence of corrosive hydrogen sulfide and fluids from the well that were being produced at extraordinary pressures—17,400 pounds per square inch—and at hellish temperatures—275 degrees.

Further, since much of the oil-producing infrastructure lies on the sea bottom under tremendous pressure that would crush any person who tried to descend there, everything from the arrays of valves called Christmas trees that sit on top of the well heads, to the steel pipes that rise up more than a mile through the turbulent loop currents to bring the oil from seafloor to platform, are custom-built. For an engineer like Inglis it was a dream-come-true, and he expected people to be suitably impressed. "Isn't this amazing?" he said over and over.

While Inglis climbed catwalks and descended deep into the depths of Thunder Horse's floats, his ears stuffed with foam plugs to ward off the whine of machinery, the Deepwater Horizon was about 300 miles off to the west boring the deepest oil well ever into the floor of the Gulf. The find, called Tiber, would be announced two months later, and it was the biggest find yet in the deep water of the Gulf. While the oil would not be easy to recover, BP executives were excited about it. They said it was of relatively light consistency, making it easier to extract and likely to produce a lot of gasoline, and they expected the field to have a long life.

That July there was a palpable sense of pride and esprit de corps around BP and its nerve center in an office park just off the Katy Freeway, West of Houston. The cooks on the Thunder Horse platform presented their visitors from England with rich, baked scones to make them feel at home. Even a severe thunderstorm, that forced the helicopter returning from Thunder Horse to circle round and round above the swamps surrounding Houma, didn't dampen Inglis's spirits.

The Gulf of Mexico was proving to be an even greater success for BP than just about anyone expected. The region was so important to the future of the company that Inglis settled in Houston with his wife Bobbye, an American, and their five children. In the 1990s, while working in Alaska, another BP stronghold, he had tragically lost his first wife in childbirth. Though he roamed the globe during the week and was often in London, he made Houston the headquarters of his Exploration and Production division, supplanting Sunbury, a drab London suburb. A crack golfer, who grew up near the famous Royal Lytham and St Annes course in northern England, host to the 2012 Open, Inglis was widely touted as Hayward's likely successor. And he was sought after for other prestigious jobs including the CEO slot at BAE Systems, the giant British defense contractor.

Heady stuff. But on the night of April 20, 2010, things would go sour for Inglis, for Hayward, and BP.

● ● ●

Within an hour of the explosion, Williams, Bertone, and Brown, along with 112 of their mates, were aboard a service ship, the Damon Bankston. Many were being treated in the Bankston's hospital ward, and the more seriously injured were being airlifted by the Coast Guard to hospitals on shore. Many of the people remained on the supply vessel for 36 hours as the seamen tried to find the 11 crewmembers who remained missing, and Coast Guard officials took statements of the survivors.

However, the rescue was far from the end of the disaster. Oil flowed from the Macondo well into the waters off Louisiana for 87 days, soiling that state's shrimping and fishing grounds, as well as its delicate marshlands. Oil would wash ashore on the beaches of Mississippi, and some would reach as far as Texas and Florida. For three months, BP's engineers, the same people who could find oil where few else on earth could and extract it from places no one else dared, couldn't manage to plug the hole they drilled in the Macondo prospect. When something went wrong they were mystified. As the oil gushed, the anger of the American public swelled to a howl, one that demanded action. And action was taken.

Every member of Congress who could remotely claim jurisdiction launched an investigation. On some days in summer 2010, there were three separate oil spill hearings in a single day on Capitol Hill. BP executives were summoned to Washington over and over to answer the questions and absorb the anger of Senators and Congressmen. President Barack Obama went looking for some ass to kick, as he famously said on June 6, 47 days into the spill. He found it at the door of BP, where he demanded a lump sum of $20 billion to compensate those whose lives had been ruined or damaged by the explosion and subsequent oil spill.

It was less than a year between Inglis's triumphant tour of Thunder Horse and the early morning of April 21, when he picked up the phone to dial Tony Hayward and tell him there was trouble in the Gulf.

The explosion, the fire, and that phone call marked the beginning of the end for both men. Hayward would be forced out just over four months later after his consistently horrendous performance as a public spokesman. Inglis, who became invisible to the outside world after the explosion, saw his post eliminated two months after that.

And it was a devastating blow for BP, the company that made its name pushing the bounds of the possible, deep under the waters of the Gulf. For BP, the Macondo blowout was yet another turning point. While it may not lead to the company's demise, it marks the end of its brief period of industry leadership and the beginning of a spell of downsizing and eating humble pie. The tragedy of the Deepwater Horizon, however, was not simply a horrible accident. It was a disaster that many say was long in the making, was foreseeable, and almost inevitable.

Only 15 years earlier, BP was a middleweight, mid-sized oil company, heavily bureaucratic, and known more for its long history and ties to the British government than for doing groundbreaking work.

In 1995, John Browne, an ambitious Cambridge University graduate, with a Stanford MBA who had spent his entire career with the company, took over as CEO. Through his BP 101 strategy of going after only huge new finds, combined with aggressive acquisitions, BP became the largest producer of oil and gas in the United States, with over 1 million barrels per day. A major reason for this success was its lead in the relentless march into deeper and deeper water. The oil found and produced far out in the Gulf became a huge growth area for the U.S. industry, which was now increasing production after two decades of decline. All of the deepwater activity in the Gulf just beyond its doorstep, enabled Houston to retain its primacy as the world's premier oil hub, even becoming a kind of Silicon Valley for the oil industry.

Browne also launched an initiative to rebrand BP as a green company, one that was "Beyond Petroleum" and an innovator in alternative energy. Under the glamorous and dynamic Browne, BP became the Goldman Sachs of the oil industry. It was elitist, innovative, and hard-charging.

That aggressive expansion and technological prowess, however, gave the leadership of BP a swagger that led them to believe they were better than others, industry officials say. The company had a long track record of industrial accidents in the United States and around the world, and had been under investigation by federal agencies including the EPA, the FBI, and OSHA for years. Initial investigations into the causes of the Deepwater Horizon explosion revealed a string of questionable decisions by BP officials and their Transocean Inc. subcontractors, as well as what appeared to be lax maintenance on crucial equipment and shortcuts to save time and money.

By the time it plugged the hole at the bottom of the Gulf, BP had become the biggest oil polluter in U.S. history, dwarfing the notorious Exxon Valdez, the oil tanker whose drunken captain ran his ship aground in Prince William Sound off Alaska, dumping its entire payload into the sea.

BP also had the poor luck of falling on its face in the worst possible place at a bad time. Pilloried in the U.S. press, BP found itself facing the fury of an inexperienced president and the scorn of its own industry. In very little time, the most daring and successful oil explorers on earth, who had managed to once be the envy of their peers, the toast of investors, and the darlings of some environmentalists, had become the most hated company in the Western world.

Chapter 2

The Oil Lord

With enough G-force to send a drink sloshing backwards, BP PLC's Gulfstream 5 roared down the runway of Moscow's Vnukovo Airport and climbed rapidly into the night sky. Soon a steward appeared bearing glasses of champagne and individual tins of caviar. The seven people on what was, in 2003, the world's top end corporate jet, gathered around a small, trim man. He offered a toast. "Here's to Russia," he said, "a country that has come so far so fast that there is no going back."

The toastmaster was John Browne, CEO of BP PLC from 1995 until 2007. He was leaving the Russian capital after a visit in September 2003. During his two days there, Browne packed in as much as a visiting head of state, a status he approached in influence. With police escorts parting traffic for his motorcade, he delivered two lectures to university students, met with Prime Minister Mikhail Kasyanov, and, with his Russian oligarch partners, hosted a lavish and triumphant party for VIPs among the gold- and silver-framed medieval icons of the Kremlin Armory.

Americans identify the unfortunate Tony Hayward as the public face of BP. But Browne, Hayward's predecessor, played a much greater role than Hayward did in making the company what it is today. During his tenure at BP he was probably the most influential chief of a major oil company and one of the world's best-respected business executives—a point underlined by his appointments to the boards of two prominent U.S. companies, Intel Corp. and Goldman Sachs.

Browne stretched BP to the limits and, possibly, beyond. He revived its exploration talents, greatly diversified its sources of oil and gas, and turned it into a deal machine. BP became the most interesting of the major oil companies. But being interesting sometimes backfires.

● ● ●

That trip to Russia crowned what turned out to be Browne's last great moment at BP—his daring joint venture deal with a group of Russian oligarchs. He was still at the height of his power and celebrity. Just days before, BP had finalized an $8.1 billion purchase of 50 percent of giant Russian producer, TNK, which the Russian businessmen had grabbed during President Boris Yeltsin's selloff of state assets. The new company would be called TNK-BP, and it would be enormously important to BP's future. By 2009, TNK-BP would account for nearly one quarter of the London giant's 4 million barrels per day output and 18 billion barrels of reserves.

Characteristic of Browne, this was a landmark deal with enormous risks. Under the Soviets, Russia's vast oil and gas resources had been off-limits to western companies. The Soviet oilmen worked hard to sustain production but, lacking the latest technology, output had declined sharply. After the fall of the Soviet Union in 1989, hard-nosed businessmen had won control of vast Russian oil fields and brought in savvy services companies such as Schlumberger Ltd. to help turn them around.

But BP's gaining a major equity stake in a Russian oil company was a coup, a first for a Western oil company. In an indication of its importance and political implications, the deal was signed in the presence of British Prime Minister Tony Blair and Russian President Vladimir Putin. The lure: Russia's oil and gas reserves are the largest of any country, and Russia's oil production of late had been outstripping that of Saudi Arabia.

Browne was a postmodern oilman who preferred opera to football and was more at home in Venice than Dallas. Born in 1948 in Hamburg, Germany, Browne was the son of a British Army officer, who later went to work for BP's predecessor, the Anglo-Iranian oil company. His mother was a concentration camp survivor of partly-Jewish heritage. The two met after the war in Hamburg, where his mother, who spoke several languages, was working for the allied forces as a translator. For much of Browne's youth, the family lived in Iran, giving their only child, who attended boarding school in England but visited on vacation, a taste for interesting and exotic places. As he relates in his entertaining and revealing autobiography, *Beyond Business*, Browne even witnessed a gigantic blowout in 1958 at Masjid-i-Suleiman, an oil field that was the cradle of the Iranian oil industry and the birthplace of what is now BP. He was captivated by a lecture on hair-raising experiences with runaway wells by an American named Myron Kinley, who had been called from Houston to put out the fire.

Browne tried to move BP, whose fields were nationalized in the twentieth century, back into Iran but didn't get far. The country's leadership proved too difficult, and BP had too much at stake in the United States to risk angering American leaders. Indeed, America, as much as anywhere, was key to Browne's career. After studying physics as an undergraduate at Cambridge, he was offered a research fellowship, a first step to an academic career. His father advised him to try business for a year, and he listened. Browne joined BP, which was just starting to develop the giant Prudhoe Bay field in Alaska. The company sent him to Anchorage where he learned about drilling wells. He proved his value early because he knew computers, a rarity in the 1960s. Working late at night on a leased Control Data Systems 6600, the world's first supercomputer that took up an entire room, he mapped reservoirs and helped BP catch up to its American competitors. His technological flair and flexible mindset enabled him to help BP hang on to, rather than sell, a field called Kuparuk, which eventually became Alaska's second largest. "I built models, starting out with punch tape; I had done a lot at Cambridge," he said in an interview in 2003. "It proved useful."

After Alaska, Browne moved to New York, where he lived in a Greenwich Village apartment originally sublet from the singer Richie Havens, and started picking up prints by David Hockney. It was the start of a lifelong interest in art collecting. Not your typical oilman, Browne wandered the city's art galleries, took a cooking course from James Beard, and, about this time, with much trepidation, visited his first gay bar. Though it was an open secret in his last years at BP, Browne didn't publicly acknowledge being gay until his resignation. In earlier years he worried that his sexual orientation would end his career in the macho oil industry. This tension between his public posture and private life eventually proved his undoing. In 2007 a former boyfriend, a young Canadian named Jeff Chevalier, sold the story of his relations with Browne to the *Mail on Sunday*, a London tabloid. Browne tried to block publication and in so doing misrepresented how he met Chevalier and was forced to resign.

While experimenting in New York, Browne developed computer simulations of subsurface oil flows. Working with BP's commercial side, he also continued to sharpen his business skills. He was fascinated with gauging the varied interests of different parties in order to work out deals. "I learned a tremendous amount about negotiating, about trying to get a deal with more than one partner," he said in an interview in 2003.

Browne's living arrangements in later life would strike many people as odd. After his father's death in 1980, he didn't want to leave his mother on her own, so he asked her to accompany him to California, where BP sent him to study for a business degree at Stanford University. She wound up living with him for the next two decades until she died in 2000. At Stanford in the 1980s she entertained his friends and became, as he puts it, "a very active member of the gang of spouses." "But I little realized then how dramatically that decision would impact my private life," he writes. Browne says he was never able to discuss his homosexuality with his mother, let alone persuade her to accept it. So her presence, he says, limited him to "occasional clandestine liaisons."

Despite the personal drawbacks, Browne's American experience gave him a professional edge over British counterparts at the still government-protected company. He was entrepreneurial and savvy about finance. In 1982 he devised a plan to sell quarter-point interests in BP's Forties field in the North Sea to small companies that wanted production income so the little guys could write off drilling costs against their taxes. The scheme earned hundreds of millions in profits for the company—big money at the time. Such gambits were unheard of in the staid British oil industry, and it took quite a bit of negotiation to mollify the British treasury which felt threatened with a huge loss of tax revenue.

● ● ●

From his early days at BP, Browne was marked out as someone who made his bosses look smart. Robert Horton, a former BP Chairman, tapped Browne to work for him as corporate treasurer in the early 1980s when Horton was CFO. He wasn't disappointed. Browne "arguably invented corporate banking as far as the U.K. was concerned," Horton said in a 2003 interview. Browne was busily inventing new and complex financial instruments (now called derivatives) for hedging oil prices and arbitraging foreign exchange. By centralizing the accounts of all BP's many business units into one treasury, a revolutionary concept, Browne forced BP's banks to slash the high fees they were charging for standby credit lines. "He had the ability to summon up all the facts and present them to much more senior people in a way that was lucid and clear," Horton says. "He would have made a terrific barrister." Word about BP's in-house "bank" got around. Lots of advice seekers on risk management came to see him, and Browne even got a call from the Governor of the Bank of England, the central bank, asking him why he was operating a bank without a license. BP quickly stopped calling his operation a bank.

Browne was always restless; he wanted to create something, not just operate existing facilities. He saw that money could be made buying and selling oil assets as well as through the traditional exploration and development process. He was more comfortable than many executives with taking risk—if he thought he understood it correctly. "If everything is cut and dried, there is no opportunity," he said. "Where there is a lot of risk, there is a wide range of values. You are always betting that you can see something that someone else can't."

He also thought there were huge advantages to be gained by getting out ahead of the pack. "If you do things first, you get quite a lot of value," he says. "Because you get to pick what you want to do rather than what is left over." At BP he always tried to be an early mover whether that was in Azerbaijan or Russia or the deep water of the Gulf of Mexico.

When Browne took charge of BP in 1995, it was far from clear that it would thrive or even survive. It still retained some of the culture and attitudes of the civil service company it had been until the 1980s. Like so much of British industry, it risked being swallowed by a bigger, more competitive rival from the United States or continental Europe. BP was a medium-sized player disparagingly known as a "two pipe" company—because it was almost completely dependent on maturing fields in the North Sea and Alaska. It didn't have the breadth or the financial clout to compete with the likes of cross-town rival Royal/Dutch Shell or Exxon.

The Kuwaiti government had tried to buy a controlling stake at a bargain price when the company was privatized in 1987, but were forced to sell down to 10 percent by the British government. When Brown took over he quickly received an approach from Cor Herkstroter, the CEO of Royal Dutch Shell, asking if he'd like to have a chat. Browne had no interest in having BP taken out by its more powerful Anglo Dutch rival, but managed to stall Herkstroter by playing along at dinners. He even gave a presentation on BP's Exploration and Production at a conference of senior Shell leaders. Years later Browne would try to take advantage of a moment of vulnerability at Shell with a takeover bid of his own that also went nowhere.

If there was any doubt that the choice was to eat or be eaten, that episode dispelled it. Browne thought he had little choice but to play the risky Merger & Acquisition (M&A) card even though BP didn't have that much to offer. Browne, who would thrive on making deals with foreign leaders of politically volatile lands, was determined to strike first and try to control the game. In a meeting in Berlin in 1996, he persuaded the board that BP had to bulk up. He argued that the company's investments in technology and research would generate bigger returns if they were spread over a far larger array of assets. He also believed that the governments which control the world's oil resources would want to do business with the biggest companies that were likely to remain in business for a long time.

When Browne surveyed the industry he thought it was full of weak players and ripe for consolidation. BP had already combined its European refining and marketing operations with Mobil's in 1996, so Browne looked to the American company for a megadeal. But Mobil's chiefs never came to a decision. When a last meeting with Mobil CEO Lou Noto at Mobil's airplane hangar in Washington in 1997 didn't produce an agreement, Browne decided to turn elsewhere.

Browne's experience had taught him that only when a company believes its prospects are bad would it be open to a takeover. After screening potential candidates, Browne rightly smelled that Chicago-based Amoco was vulnerable and looking for a way out of its predicament. The company had had little success in finding new oil reserves, an area where BP excelled. In addition, BP was already talking to the company about a chemical joint venture, a BP executive says. So it was natural to think about widening the scope of the talks. In February 1998, Browne dialed Larry Fuller, the CEO of Amoco, and asked about his plans for the future of the Chicago-based descendent of the old Standard Oil. Oil prices were in freefall and most companies were struggling to make ends meet. Spreading research investments and know-how over a bigger range of assets could help, Browne maintained. "It seems to me it's a good time for a few oil companies to get together," Browne said to Fuller. Two days later the pair sat across from each other at John F. Kennedy Airport in New York, the first in a series of meetings—many in a private room at the Pont de la Tour restaurant in London.

● ● ●

Browne and Fuller were as different as their companies. Browne is small-framed, with thick brown hair and a soft voice spoken in a posh British accent. Fuller is ruddy with a bulbous face, a head with thinning white hair, and a deep, resonant voice that's tinged with a Midwest twang. As much as Browne's BP was "entrepreneurial," a place where unit managers had real power over their operations and risk-taking was considered a strength, Fuller's Amoco was a top-down shop where decisions were taken slowly and caution was a watchword. Some Amoco employees were displeased by the deal. They thought Fuller was selling at the bottom of the market.

The Making of an Oil Patch Power

John Browne's
deal machine ...

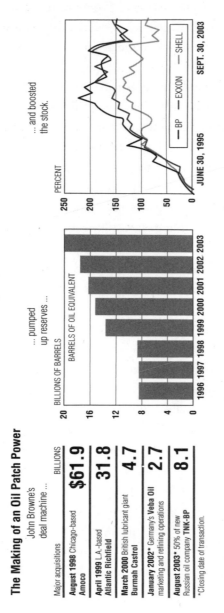

Major acquisitions	BILLIONS
August 1998 Chicago-based **Amoco**	**$61.9**
April 1999 L.A.-based **Atlantic Richfield**	**31.8**
March 2000 British lubricant giant **Burmah Castrol**	**4.7**
January 2002* Germany's **Veba Oil** marketing and refining operations	**2.7**
August 2003* 50% of new Russian oil company **TNK-BP**	**8.1**

*Closing date of transaction.

... pumped
up reserves ...

BILLIONS OF BARRELS

BARRELS OF OIL EQUIVALENT

1996 1997 1998 1999 2000 2001 2002 2003

... and boosted
the stock.

PERCENT

— BP — EXXON — SHELL

JUNE 30, 1995   SEPT. 30, 2003

BP CEO John Browne went on an acquisition spree from 1998 through 2003. The purchases boosted the company's reserves and market value and launched it into the top tier of global oil companies.

Source: Stanley Reed, "The Oil Lord," *BusinessWeek,* October 27, 2003.

Fuller alluded to the differences in an e-mail to his employees announcing the merger. "I feel—as you probably do, too—that we are losing something of our heritage in this transaction," he wrote. "There is some truth to that, but in return we are becoming part of an industry giant."

The combination would give BP a range of new assets to play with, including additional leases in the Gulf of Mexico and a big position in Trinidad. This created a marvelous platform for supplying liquefied natural gas, a fast-growing industrial fuel, to the United States. As the negotiations came to a climax, Browne was able to play hardball—demanding a majority on the board and a single company headquartered in London—and forcing Fuller to cede on just about every point. The $62 billion deal was the largest industrial merger to date, and it launched an era of consolidation in the oil industry. It was Browne's "coup of all time," said John Lichtblau, chairman of the New York-based Petroleum Industry Research Association, the day the deal was announced.

The Amoco deal had barely gone through when Lee Raymond at Exxon one-upped it by buying the coveted Mobil Corp. Other deals followed. In 1999, Thierry Desmarest, the brainy CEO of France's Total, waged a long, bitter, and successful takeover battle to gain Paris rival Elf; while Chevron swallowed weakened American sister Texaco.

Browne kept on acquiring. Not long after the Amoco deal was completed Browne received a call from Mike Bowlin, CEO of the Atlantic Richfield Co. The medium-sized Los Angeles-based company had decided that it couldn't compete in an era of low oil prices and wanted to join forces with BP. On April 1, 1999, just four months after the Amoco acquisition was final, BP announced it would buy ARCO for $32 billion. With the deal, BP would get ARCO's fields on Alaska's North Slope, leaving the combined company to pump 70 percent of the state's oil.

The U.S. government, however, didn't see the concentration of the country's energy assets in the hands of a foreign company as a benefit.

The Federal Trade Commission sued to block the merger and only relented when BP agreed to sell ARCO's Alaska holdings to Phillips Petroleum Co. for $7 billion. The settlement left BP with ARCO's west coast refining business and some natural gas fields in Asia, but wound up being mostly a dud for Browne.

Browne was operating in an era of low prices that is easily forgotten more than 10 years later. In the late 1990s, a barrel of crude dipped to $10, and some industry CEOs thought they might remain at those levels for a long time. Company profitability, which is very closely tied to prices, plummeted. The industry, not just BP, cut thousands of jobs including engineers and other key technical personnel. A lot of key brainwork in the industry is now done by service companies such as Schlumberger and Halliburton.

The low price environment shaped Browne's outlook, probably for the rest of his career. He was the most ruthless cost-cutter of all in his early days. Browne set ambitious integration and cost-cutting goals for the Amoco and Arco mergers—promising $4 billion in savings by 2002—and then he proceeded to exceed them. In November 1999 he said BP would be a year early in delivering the $2 billion in savings at Amoco and by the end of 2000 had met the $2 billion in target cuts from ARCO. BP earned $14.2 billion in 2000.

The Amoco deal gave added credence to Browne's growing reputation as an industry visionary. Browne's Russian deal, if not widely copied, was certainly groundbreaking. He was also an early investor in China, establishing lasting ties with the fastest growing oil consumer, and was a pioneer in Azerbaijan and Libya, two promising producer countries. "He brings great intellectual capacity and strategic sense and an ability to think in the future tense," said Daniel Yergin, now Chairman of IHS CERA and the author of *The Prize*, the definitive history of the oil industry, at the time of the TNK merger.

● ● ●

Browne kept looking for ways to distinguish BP from other oil companies, which in the public's mind were all pretty much the same. This quest for distinction motivated BP to adopt a controversial new identity, rebranding itself "Beyond Petroleum." Browne figured out early on in the mid-1990s that climate change was an issue of growing importance, and he wanted BP to be a player in the debate, not a punching bag. He decided that if scientists were right, and that global warming was being caused by carbon emissions then "our industry was unsustainable in its current form." He sounded out scientists, nongovernmental organizations, and political leaders, including then-President Bill Clinton. In May 1997, in a speech given outdoors on a sweltering day at Stanford University near San Francisco, BP "broke ranks with the rest of the oil industry," as Browne put it, and acknowledged the threat of climate change.

"The time to consider the policy dimensions of climate change is not when the link between greenhouse gases and climate change is conclusively proven, but when the possibility cannot be discounted and is taken seriously by the society of which we are part," Browne said. "We in BP have reached that point."

Browne realized that an oil company proclaiming itself "green" might provoke howls of skepticism. He needed real steps, not just talk. So he went to some of the oil industry's most effective critics for help. One was Fred Krupp, head of the Environmental Defense Fund, a nongovernmental organization that had a big role in halting the construction of the Trans Alaska Pipeline in the early 1970s. Krupp helped BP set up an internal carbon trading scheme. Browne committed BP to a series of goals, including reducing the company's carbon emissions to 10 percent below the 1990 level by 2010. Such commitments spawned some ambitious projects, such as a $4 billion gas field called In Salah that BP has developed with the Algerian national oil company, Sonatrach, deep in the Sahara Desert. In a test of a technology called carbon capture and storage, excess carbon dioxide is removed from the gas at the field and, instead of being vented into the atmosphere, injected deep into the ground. The developers say this activity is the equivalent of taking 200,000 cars off the road.

"It was a big deal," said Eileen Claussen, the president of the Pew Center on Global Climate Change. Claussen discussed early drafts of the speech with Browne and told him he'd have to do more than talk to win her over. "A speech is good, but you've got to do what you say you're going to do." Browne, she said, followed through. The company worked hard to reduce its carbon emissions while simultaneously investing in alternative energy technology and companies.

"Beyond Petroleum" itself came along later. After his acquisition spree, Browne wanted a brand and identity to unify the various companies. It was also an opportunity to give BP a new face, different from the conventional image of the industry, which he says was "old-fashioned and dirty, and still secretive and manipulative." That was no longer what BP was like, he says. "It was to be a competitively profitable force for good, which valued top-class, safe operational performance, innovation, progress and environmental leadership."

Two units of advertising giant WPP were hired to do the work. Landor & Associates came up with the green and yellow flower or "Helios" logo, which symbolized the sun and BP's ability to provide a range of energy sources other than oil. Ogilvy & Mather came up with the "Beyond Petroleum" tag line.

Company executives weren't unanimously with Browne on the idea. They feared that BP could easily be painted as a hypocrite for claiming they were "beyond" their core product. The CEO went ahead anyway. His timing was impeccable. Global warming had become the single barometer by which people were measuring a company's environmental credentials. And BP told the world it was with them.

The ensuing advertising push was wildly popular. It won two "Campaign of the Year" awards from PR Week and an "Effie" gold medal for "sustained success" from the American Marketing Association. And industry insiders say BP was suddenly attracting the top talent from engineering schools around the world, young people who earlier wouldn't have wanted to work for an oil company.

There were certainly detractors. A website called CorpWatch called the campaign "Beyond Preposterous," and *Mother Jones* magazine pointed out that only one-tenth of one percent of BP's sales went beyond petroleum. Overall, however, BP's position, and aggressive marketing of it, opened the door for other companies to publicly recognize that climate change was a threat. Browne succeeded in making himself and BP pivotal figures in the corporate environmental movement and darlings of global warming advocates.

"John Browne was the single most important business figure on climate change in the 1990s," said Paul Bledsoe, a climate and media expert who served in the Interior Department and Clinton White House at the time. "After his speech, it became much harder for other companies to deny the science with impunity."

● ● ●

Just as Browne rode the environmental zeitgeist to success, he also seized the opportunities offered by the political upheavals of technological advances of the late 1990s. The fall of the Soviet Union, the rise of China, and technological changes, such as the ability to drill and produce oil in deeper water depths, were creating heretofore unknown opportunities. The Cold War was over and the Soviet Union had been swept aside. Governments needed revenue. Not only Russia but also former satellites such as Azerbaijan and Kazakhstan, with troves of oil and gas of their own, were opening up. With the civil war in Angola winding down, another potential BP stronghold looked ripe for exploitation.

Advances in computing technology were making it easier to map potential oil- and gas-bearing rocks deep in the earth. That meant the risk that a multimillion-dollar investment in an exploration well was less likely to come up as a dry hole. Now was the time to sell older fields and go after growth, he concluded.

Following the ExxonMobil deal, BP's European marketing joint venture with Mobil unraveled, leaving BP without a lubricant brand. So BP bought Burmah Castrol, a company which had helped finance BP nearly a century before, to gain its Castrol lubricants brand.

The deal spree propelled BP into what Browne wanted it to be—one of the big three in the industry with ExxonMobil and Royal Dutch Shell. The Amoco purchase also sealed BP's fate as a company highly dependent on how it fared in the United States. It also brought new leases in the Gulf of Mexico and added knowledge of the area, where BP was already moving out into the deep water, thinking it saw a huge opportunity there that wasn't appreciated by its rivals.

Being the leader of a company with so much breadth and financial clout was a whole different experience from running a middleweight a few years before, Browne said at the time. He doubted that the old BP would have had the credibility to pull off its Russia venture. The added clout had its personal satisfactions too. Browne was first knighted in 1998 and then, in 2001, was elevated to the House of Lords. He could gain access almost anywhere: from the Kremlin, to the Forbidden City in Beijing, to the White House, or to the cigar-smoking tent that California Governor Arnold Schwarzenegger had erected outside the state capitol building in Sacramento.

For journalists, Browne had the virtue of being accessible. Always impeccably dressed, he liked to hold court in his modernistic office, decorated with avant-garde art and the hand-carved furniture of the Queen's grandson, Viscount Linley. Company rules were waived, and visitors were permitted and even encouraged to smoke in his office. Puffing on a Cuban cigar, he would regale his visitors in his plummy voice with hilarious stories of his jockeying with other industry big shots. Lee Raymond, the formidable Chairman and CEO of ExxonMobil, apparently reveled in snubbing the diminutive London upstart. Ali Al-Naimi, the Saudi Oil Minister, was a source of exasperation. "Ali" had earned lasting scorn by wasting BP's and other oil companies' time and money in a protracted bid for natural gas exploration acreage that wound up producing nothing for anyone.

For the favored, there were parties at Browne's apartment that sparkled with wit from the likes of the comedian Rory Bremner or afternoons watching tennis at Wimbledon in a party that might include an ambassador or two, a Downing Street advisor, and a sprinkling of senior BP executives. Browne usually came for the women's finals. After a sumptuous lunch featuring stone crab claws and other delicacies, he would nod off while players such as Venus and Serena Williams swatted the ball back and forth at center court.

● ● ●

Browne basked in his fame. But not all aspects of the takeovers were going well. Despite having spent years in the United States and now having the largest part of his business there, Browne and his colleagues in top management never seemed to quite come to grasp how to do business there. One problem: None of Browne's key lieutenants wanted to move to the United States. That would be too far from the boss. For a man who preached the need to understand and engage in the communities where he does business, it was a massive oversight. He followed the takeovers with cost cutting that may have pleased Wall Street but damaged the company's core. Amoco's executive ranks were largely cleaned out, depriving BP of talent it might have been able to use. And Browne admits that rebranding all the U.S. Amoco gas stations with the BP logo was "a huge mistake" that jeopardized customer allegiance.

What's clear is that Browne and BP fell short in understanding and properly managing the U.S. refinery network that came with Amoco. The worst of many signs of this failure to provide strong management was the blast at the former Amoco Texas City refinery in 2005 that killed 15 people and injured scores of others. That incident began the long slide in BP's reputation and put the company permanently in the sights of U.S. regulators. In that sense, what seemed like a no-brainer deal proved to have a significant downside for BP.

Still, there is no question that Browne transformed BP from a company largely dependent on maturing assets in the West to one focused on emerging growth areas such as Azerbaijan, Angola, Russia and the deep water of the Gulf of Mexico. By the early twenty-first century the company was no longer a two pipe outfit, but a giant that, through acquisitions and relationships with foreign governments, had more than doubled its production to 3.8 million barrels per day.

His legacy, such as it is, may turn out to be more the relationships BP forged with emerging countries than the mergers in the United States. In private conversations Browne was clearly far more interested in trying to figure out whether his Russian partners would be able to survive the latest power struggles in the Kremlin, or the motivations of the Chinese leadership, than in western M&A deals. He relished the challenge of cross-cultural negotiations, and always went the last mile to strike the deal, putting on an overly large academic gown at a Russian university to the amusement of his entourage, swallowing a sheep's eye in Azerbaijan, and playing high-level hide-and-seek across Libya in search of Muammar Qaddafi.

● ● ●

It was 2005 when Browne, to the dismay of his pilot, allowed his plane to be directed to mysterious coordinates in the Libyan desert. Upon landing, Browne and his Arab affairs advisor Sir Mark Allen, a former higher-up in the British intelligence agency MI6, were made to cool their heels at a hotel for a night before being taken on another trip to Muammar Qaddafi's tent. There, swatting away flies with a fan made of birch twigs, he worked out the principles of BP's re-entry to Libya. The deal, finalized after Browne's resignation in 2007, gave BP a swath of offshore exploration acreage the size of Belgium.

But that deal also led to controversy when it emerged in summer 2010 that Allen had lobbied the British government to conclude a prisoner-transfer agreement with the Libyan government that would have enabled Abdel Basset Ali Al-Megrahi, the only person ever convicted for the 1988 Pan Am 103 airliner bombing over Scotland, which killed 270 people, 189 of them Americans, to serve out his sentence in a Libyan prison. BP said such a deal would be helpful in furthering its interests in Libya. In the end, the Scottish government released Al-Megrahi on humanitarian grounds in August 2009 on the belief he was close to dying of cancer. Nevertheless, the appearance that BP would put grubby oil deals ahead of holding Muammar Al Qaddafi's agent to account further blackened the company's image in the U.S.

While he enjoyed cutting deals with potentates, Browne could also be tough on them when he felt the need. In 2001, pressed by non-governmental organizations, he decided to publish specifics on BP's operations in Angola, one of the company's strongholds, including the payment of a $111 million signature bonus. Oil companies routinely pay these large lump sums upon signing leases and they present an obvious opportunity for corruption.

Sonangol, the Angolan national oil company, shot back with a letter accusing BP of "seriously violating the conditions of legal contracts." Browne was summoned to the impoverished capital, Luanda, to see an angry President Jose Eduardo dos Santos, who made clear that he could kick BP out of the country. A BP executive present in Angola at the time said the company ran the risk of being tossed. But Browne held his ground.

In business terms Browne will likely be best remembered as the executive who brought financial acumen and big time deal making to the stodgy oil business. When he spoke, people listened. The question being asked now is did he also sow the seeds of BP's near self-immolation by building too fast and paying too little attention to operational details.

BP insiders say that Browne's experience at Intel and in Silicon Valley inspired him to try to push BP to grow at a speed more appropriate for a technology company than an oil giant, whose projects require years if not decades to come to fruition. This drive to be a growth company led to embarrassment and investor anger in 2002 when BP admitted that its production growth would be 3 percent rather than its 5.5 percent annual target. The admission knocked down BP's stock price and set off a storm of criticism from the investment community. Executives at rival companies privately delighted in seeing the previously untouchable Browne scrape his knee. While the hit to BP's earnings was small—perhaps $100 million—the damage in the investment community was major. CFO Byron Grote said BP took a long-lasting hit to its "reputation as a company for meeting its targets."

Other BP insiders wondered whether Browne should have ever set production targets. After all it was an oil company, where production is hostage to many factors including the price of oil, host governments, and long investment lead times.

In a conversation in 2003 Browne downplayed this episode, saying BP was foolish to allow itself to become hostage to a single statistic. But the snafu, which revealed that pressured managers were feeding flawed information into headquarters, goaded him into a thorough review of the whole organization. The conclusion: BP still had a lot of work to do in forging its various parts into a smooth-running machine. Employees of the acquired companies felt like stepchildren. Browne responded to the missed production targets fiasco with a campaign focused around a much derided document called the Green Book, which called for greater accountability but, in the view of critics, meant hiring more accountants and other support staff, adding billions to overhead.

Detractors also said that Browne was such a powerful figure within BP that the company had trouble grooming successors. One investment banker said that Browne's influence was so strong at the company that he could tell whether he was in the headquarters building on St. James Square in London by whether people were on their toes or not. During Browne's tenure BP's modern, glass-walled offices had the feel of a court. Browne was dubbed "The Sun King." It was almost required for young, promising executives to work for him for around 18 months as a "turtle," a kind of personal assistant who did everything from coordinating his schedule to making sure he landed the souvenirs he coveted on foreign trips. Hayward, Dudley, and Inglis were all turtles.

Whether the king was serious about preparing an heir was an open question. Some of the most plausible CEO candidates left or were driven out of the company during Browne's time, allowing substantially younger people, who were no threat, to fill their shoes. Hayward and other potential CEO candidates were given big responsibilities, but they remained in the shadow of the boss, who always seemed to take charge when there was a crisis. Such lack of preparation may have contributed to Hayward's poor performances as a public spokesman in the United States during the agonizing period when the company was unable to shut down the flow of crude from the spewing Macondo well into the Gulf of Mexico. "They just weren't battle-hardened," says one former BP executive about Hayward and his generation.

Browne's closest advisor was not even an employee of the company. Dick Balzer, an American management consultant, worked at BP almost fulltime, coaching Browne on leadership and nurturing his fragile self-confidence. Balzer would carefully watch Browne's performance and give him feedback on it later. On the return trip from Moscow the two sat together engaged in quiet conversation.

Browne could be very demanding, associates say. He lived entirely for BP and set a standard not everyone could live up to. One former executive said that more was demanded of people at BP than at other companies. At periodic reviews Browne would grill his lieutenants.

"What did you do? Why did you fail? What are you going to do differently?"

Senior managers all had performance contracts: One page documents spelling out metrics such as how many wells they were to drill, how many barrels they were to find, safety statistics and so forth. "He had an incredible memory. If you told him something the year before and then changed your tune, he would pick up on it. These were often unpleasant experiences," this person said.

Throughout his tenure at BP, Browne was obsessed with ExxonMobil, a substantially larger company by market value. Browne was well aware that ExxonMobil's performance outstripped BP's on several fronts, including return on capital.

● ● ●

One area where BP was beating the competition was in adding reserves—a trend that should have allowed BP's production to grow faster in the future. Under Browne, BP staked its future on five new areas: Azerbaijan, Trinidad, Angola, a liquid natural gas (LNG) project in Indonesia, and the deep water off the Gulf of Mexico. Russia added a sixth card to BP's hand. But it would also be a source of trouble for Browne's successor, Tony Hayward.

The 2003 Russia deal grew out of a troubled $570 million investment for a 10 percent stake in a company called Sidanco. BP had made the investment through an oligarch named Vladimir Potanin, who looked like a good partner but turned out to be a poor choice. BP soon found itself caught in a fight between Potanin and the oligarchs who wound up being its partners in TNK-BP. In 1999, Sidanco's key asset, a production unit called Chernogorneft, was declared bankrupt in a Siberian court and sold for a song to BP's current Russian partners. After a lot of haggling, BP reached a deal: Sidanco's seized assets would be returned, and BP would up its stake to 25 percent. BP also agreed to consider buying a stake in TNK, the oil assets controlled by Fridman and his partners.

Why join forces with people, who once ripped you off? Both BP executives and Fridman, who is now Chairman of the Russian company, say the maneuvering, in which BP was mostly an innocent bystander, brought the two groups together. "When you go into battle with someone you get to know them pretty well," said a BP executive.

Browne, already a Lord, and Fridman were unlikely partners. Browne, despite his innovative nature, had succeeded through working for one large corporation his entire life. Fridman, who is very conscious of his status as a member of the Jewish minority, had taken a necessarily unconventional route. Unlike many Jews, who had fled the Soviet Union, he stayed. He started a range of entrepreneurial if fringe businesses such as buying up theater tickets to sell on the black market and window washing. Always opportunistic, he bought multibillion-dollar businesses cheap during Yeltsin's privatizations.

Fridman says Browne was "one of the smartest men I ever met in my life" but not easy to work with. "My English is not good enough to talk to John Browne," he says. "It is hard to get what is on his mind." By contrast, he says Browne's successor, Tony Hayward, was "a pretty straight guy." Hayward, who joined the TNK-BP board after his departure from BP, "is much more friendly," Fridman says, although "sometimes a bit emotional."

BP's dealmakers also judged, perhaps incorrectly, that Fridman would be a more malleable partner than other oil entrepreneurs operating in Russia. The heads of Lukoil and Yukos may have had better assets, but they viewed themselves as professional oil executives and would have resisted the management dictates of an international company, BP thought. They were wise to avoid Yukos, whose controlling shareholder, Mikhail Khodorkovsky, wound up being jailed by Putin.

Browne was well aware of the risks in Russia. He liked to say that it was clear that Russia would have a strong oil industry but less so what the role was for foreign companies in it. At times it looked as if

BP might be snookered again. In 2008, Dudley, then TNK-BP's CEO, was driven from the country by a barrage of lawsuits, tax probes, difficulties obtaining work permits, and other legal pressures that became a hallmark of the acrimonious partnership's battles over management control and investment direction. One Russian court even barred Dudley from performing his job for two years for allegedly violating local labor laws.

By the numbers, the venture inked by Browne and Fridman in 2003 has been extraordinarily successful. TNK-BP's production has grown faster than that of any other Russian oil company, and the two sides have been taking roughly $2 billion a year in dividends. BP has easily earned back its investment.

Those fat payouts weren't enough to keep the relationship from going rancid. On his 2003 visit, Browne told Russian university students that BP had been responsible for "some very bad colonial behavior. That must never happen again." Yet, even BP people admit that the company wound up behaving in a colonialist way in Russia. Management meetings turned into screaming battles. At a board meeting in November 2007, the two sides found themselves far apart on dividends with Dudley arguing that with oil prices down it made more sense to cut the dividends and plow what cash there was into fields and equipment. The Russian partners were having none of that, and they also bridled at BP's vetoing proposals for TNK-BP to invest overseas. BP told the partners they could add more value in Russia. Another practice that infuriated the Russians was BP's parking of second-rate people at the Russian company.

A settlement was reached in September 2008 that gave the Russians much of what they wanted, including a Russian CEO. But BP executives say that the deal gives BP better protection of its 50 percent stake. Despite the jockeying, BP retains its position, giving it a unique status in Russia for a foreign oil company. Putin has not revoked his blessing despite a hardening of Russian attitudes toward foreign oil companies. There is no way the Russians would permit a 50 percent stake in such a venture today, and BP's rival, Royal Dutch Shell, was forced to give up its control of the Sakhalin II project in the Russian far east to Gazprom in 2006.

When Dudley was tapped as CEO of BP itself on July 27, 2010, he received a congratulatory call from the most important partner, Mikhail Fridman, jocularly promising him he would have no trouble working in Russia anymore.

Chapter 3

Agents of Empire

A glance backward into BP's past is needed to understand how damaging the Gulf of Mexico debacle is for the company and to gauge its chances for recovery. Among the major oil companies BP stands out as an explorer. It is also a company that has proven that it can adjust to very serious shocks, including the loss of most of its sources of oil. BP, or at least its predecessor, the Anglo-Persian Oil Co., helped create an oil industry in the Middle East, now by far the most important oil region in the world. BP and its precursors were in on the discovery of many of the world's monster oil fields, including Kirkuk and Rumaila in Iraq, and Burgan in Kuwait. Almost all of that oil was taken away from BP in the wave of nationalizations in the 1970s.

During the nationalization movement that started in the 1950s, BP's leaders directed their explorers westward, away from the volatile Middle East. Britain and Europe were never going to have the oil to sustain a major oil company for more than a brief period. BP had to keep looking for new reserves—or oil in the ground. It was always trying to steal a march on its competitors, most of which were better funded. In the 1970s, BP participated in the discovery of Prudhoe Bay in Alaska and the Forties Field in the North Sea off Britain. And then it moved to the Gulf of Mexico in the mid-1980s. It was just beginning to reap the harvest of a long and clever campaign when the Macondo disaster struck.

● ● ●

Unlike ExxonMobil, whose roots go back to John D. Rockefeller's tight control of trade in oil in the nineteenth century, BP's origins lie in a roll of the dice that discovered oil in Iran in the early twentieth century. That considerable achievement opened up the Middle East's vast troves of cheap oil, without which we could not live the way we do now. BP's Middle Eastern experience also left the company with a colonial legacy that still works against it today.

The person BP hails as its founder, William Knox D'Arcy, was an entrepreneur and a speculator. D'Arcy had moved to Australia as a youth and made a sizeable fortune out of a gold mine. He later returned to England, where he lived a luxurious and flamboyant life with a town house on Grosvenor Square in London and two country estates, one where he took friends shooting. He married an actress, named Nina Boucicault, and the pair entertained lavishly, even hiring Enrico Caruso, the Pavarotti of his day, to sing at parties.

People looking for financial backers for their schemes came to D'Arcy, who was always on the lookout for new ventures. He had become intrigued with oil and gas prospects in Persia through the writings of a French geologist named Jacques de Morgan. When approached by a member of the Persian ruler's entourage, he was ready to take a chance. In 1901, he managed to obtain, through intermediaries, what in hindsight seems an extraordinary deal from the ruler of Persia, Muzaffar-al-din Shah, who was desperate for cash.

D'Arcy gained an exclusive, 60-year concession from the Shah to find and export oil and gas. In exchange, the country's ruler was to receive 30,000 sterling in cash, shares in a company to be formed, and 16 percent of the profits. In what would become an oil industry tradition, the insider who brokered the deal, General Antoine Kitabgi, "secured in a very thorough manner the support of all the Shah's principle ministers and courtiers, not even forgetting the personal servant who brings his Majesty his pipe and morning coffee," according to the Britain's envoy in Tehran. He took 10,000 pounds for his trouble.

By today's standards, where governments take upwards of 90 percent of oil revenues, D'Arcy's terms were amazing. But he was heading into the near unknown. Geologists believed Iran's Zagros Mountains were formed of folds in the earth's crust, called anticlines, and had a good chance of having trapped oil. Still, Persia was difficult going, and no commercial oil deposits had been found there. D'Arcy never visited Persia himself. Instead, he hired an engineer named George Reynolds to try out his theories. Reynolds assembled an international party, including rig workers from Baku in what is now Azerbaijan, where the closest oil fields to Iran were then found.

• • •

In those early days of the industry, oil prospectors had to be a hearty breed to even survive. Reynolds had been employed by the Indian Public Works Department before moving on to exploring for Royal Dutch Shell in Sumatra. This is how an official BP history describes him: "Tough, hardworking and self-reliant, he was a competent if mostly self-trained geologist. Just as importantly he was a natural linguist and a good horseman with a talent for getting things done."

The search for oil in Persia drained D'Arcy's fortune. Reynolds and others working for him drilled in various sites beginning in 1902, finding some oil but not commercial quantities. Working in barren lands, they struggled with temperatures up to 120 degrees, bad water, and tribal bandits, who had to be bought off again and again. In 1904, D'Arcy, who had spent something on the order of 235,000 pounds, more than 10 times what he anticipated, cast about for help. "Every purse has its limits," he wrote in 1903. "And I can see the limits of my own."

After being turned down by various parties including the British Admiralty, the Rothschilds, and Rockefeller's Standard Oil, he brought in Burmah Oil, then Britain's second largest oil company after Shell. Ironically Browne would later buy it. Burmah, which was run by a wily and parsimonious group of Scottish businessmen, who had made their money in the Far East, was producing oil in Burma but needed more reserves to meet its contract with the British Admiralty for 350,000 barrels a year in fuel. D'Arcy retained a large stake, but the Scots took over management and control. They also assured themselves of the backing of the British government, which was jockeying with Russia for influence in the region in what is known as "The Great Game."

New capital didn't mean instant success. By early 1908 Burmah's patience was exhausted and the company sent Reynolds a letter threatening to pull the plug. But as the missive wound its slow way to him Reynolds was finally drilling in a place in Southwest Persia that would bring success. It was called Masjid-i-Suleiman for the remains found there of an ancient fire temple. A youthful John Browne, perhaps in short pants, had clambered on these stones. On May 26, 1908, Reynolds struck oil. The oil, found at a depth of about a thousand feet, shot up into the air, while the sulphurous gas choked the drillers.

That discovery and subsequent finds in Persia became the foundation of the business that eventually evolved into modern day BP. The gusher, discovered by what may have been the last well Reynolds could have drilled, bailed everyone out. Shares in a new company, called the Anglo-Persian Oil Co., were sold to investors in April, 1909. D'Arcy wound up making a profit of about 50 million pounds in today's terms. Reynolds, who repeatedly clashed with Burmah's managers, was fired in 1911 with only a modest payoff.

Anglo-Persian's prosperity didn't last for long. Serious capital was required to build the refineries and export system required to develop Iran into an oil hub. The heavyweight backing needed came in the form of Winston Churchill, who became First Lord of the Admiralty in 1911. Churchill believed that the navy should convert its fleet from coal to oil, and he argued that Britain needed to back another oil producer in order to make sure it was not completely dependent on Shell, which otherwise might be able to set monopoly prices. Being partly Dutch-owned, Shell, Churchill argued, spuriously but effectively, was subject to German influence. The Navy gave Anglo-Persian a contract to supply 40 million barrels of oil over 20 years starting in 1914. And the British government injected 2 million pounds for a majority stake.

When World War I broke out, the company became a key supplier to the navy. Output rose from 200,000 barrels in 1913 to 3.5 million barrels by 1917. In an indication of how much oil consumption and production has increased, the latter number represents a little less than a day's production in Iran today. During the War, Anglo-Persian saw the chance to acquire a distribution network called British Petroleum which had been seized as enemy property because it was German owned. Anglo-Persian acquired the company's assets in 1917 but it did not adopt the name until 1954.

Persia, now named Iran, became even more important to the western allies in World War II. The British were worried that German influence in Tehran would threaten their fuel supply, so they invaded, occupying the area near the oil fields. Production was ramped up to 345,000 barrels per day. Equipment shipped all the way from the United States was used to soup up the big refinery at Abadan to produce high octane fuel for fighters and bombers. Now called Anglo-Iranian, the company mostly depended on Iranian oil until 1951.

We think of companies like BP, ExxonMobil, and Royal Dutch Shell as immensely powerful, and they are; but today's versions of these companies are nowhere near as dominant as they were in the middle decades of the twentieth century. In 1950, for instance, mostly due to its positions in the Middle East, BP's share of total world oil reserves was an astounding 23 percent. It fell to 13 percent in 1970, but that was still a huge number. In hindsight, those years were the zenith of the majors. They controlled 63 percent of world oil reserves in 1970, when the seismic shift in control had just begun.

As a company with almost all of its oil reserves and production outside of its home base, BP was probably the major most exposed to the wave of oil nationalism. A new generation of leaders and advisors in oil producing countries, influenced by the post-World War II anti-colonialist movement, figured out that they deserved a much better deal from the oil companies that operated in their land. Oil also became an extremely emotional issue, perhaps exceeding even its economic importance. Politicians portrayed it as the nation's blood, the national patrimony, with great success. For western oil companies the substance they produced and traded became political dynamite. By the early twenty-first century national oil companies in places such as Saudi Arabia, Iran, and Venezuela controlled 65 percent of the world's reserves, though they still needed the international companies to help produce the oil.

It was hardly surprising that Anglo-Iranian became the target of one of the first of these great nationalist backlashes. The clash between Anglo-Iranian and Mohammed Mossadegh, an eccentric but very popular Iranian politician, was protracted, messy and damaging to both sides. Western oilmen, not always the best readers of political trends, thought the host countries owed them a huge debt for developing their resources, while local politicians, who saw a source of revenues and power, argued that what was in the ground belonged to their nations.

In the post-war world, the powerful and privileged position enjoyed by Anglo-Iranian was no longer tenable, regardless of legalities. The world was changing. Governments such as those of Saudi

Arabia and Venezuela were asserting greater control over their natural resources. The company's lock on the precious resource grated on the Iranian populace, forcing even the Iranian politicians in Britain's pocket to seek a better deal.

Anglo-Iranian resisted making concessions. Between 1945 and 1950, the royalties it paid to Iran were roughly a third of its profits, and lower than the taxes it paid to the British government. The company treated its Iranian employees as second class at best. An Iranian observer described the enormous gap between the conditions the Iranian employees lived under and the luxuries of the British management of the company: "Wages were fifty cents a day. There was no sick leave, no vacation pay, no disability compensation. The workers lived in a shantytown called Kahgazabad, or Paper City, without running water or electricity; let alone luxuries such as ice boxes or fans. . . . In the British section of Abadan there were lawns, rose beds, tennis courts; swimming pools and clubs."

As Stephen Kinzer tells the story in *All the Shah's Men*, a backlash built, leading to an epic power struggle that in the simplest terms pitted the Iranian people against the company and Great Britain. The company's Chairman, Sir William Fraser, offered Iran modest concessions in 1949, including a floor on royalty payments. The Iranians wanted greater say over the company's management and a look at the books. Fraser flatly refused. In the same year the Shah Mohammed Riza Pahlavi rigged an election to the *Majlis* or Iranian parliament. Violent protests followed. The opposition crystallized around a National Front led by Mohammed Mossadegh.

The nationalists and religious leaders joined together in a campaign to nationalize the oil company. Huge crowds turned out to support the move. The moderate Prime Minister Ali Razmara was assassinated, removing a powerful force for restraint from the scene. The youthful Shah, who was to crumble like a gingerbread man during the Islamic Revolution in the late 1970s, proved equally ineffectual in this early test. The British Ambassador offered a 50/50 split, but it was too late.

The *Majlis*, led by Mossadegh, voted to nationalize the Anglo-Iranian Oil Company in late April 1951.

Compromise was in the interests of both sides. The company had a great deal to lose, but so did Mossadegh's government, though he didn't seem to understand the dangers. Anglo-Persian had skills, and its main owner, the British government, was still powerful in the international sphere. But the personalities involved proved intractable. Anglo-Iranian's Chairman, Sir William Fraser, was a "famously obstinate Scotsman, who hated the idea of compromise." His opponent was one of the most colorful and tragic characters of the wave of post-war anti-colonialism.

Mossadegh, the son of a *Qajar* princess, had spent decades opposing the governments of the day and going in and out of exile. By the time he became a world figure, as Prime Minister in the 1950s, he was in his late 60s. He had a long aristocratic face, droopy basset hound eyes, and a habit of bursting into tears and even fainting at emotional moments. But he was a spellbinding orator, incorruptible, and enormously popular.

His appeal went far beyond Iran. When he visited the United States to make his case, he cut a sympathetic figure on television, comparing the Anglo-Iranian case to the American struggle for independence. The *New York Daily News* dubbed him "Mossy." *Time* made him Man of the Year in 1951, saying: "In his plaintive, singsong voice he gabbled a defiant challenge that sprang out of a hatred and envy almost incomprehensible to the West."

Mossy found a perfect foil in Anglo-Iranian. In a speech to the U.N. Security Council he said: "Our greatest natural asset is oil. This should be the source of work and food for the population of Iran. As now organized the petroleum industry has contributed practically nothing to the well-being of the people or to the technical progress or industrial development of my country."

In 1951, he became Prime Minister, riding a nationalist wave often expressed in the form of violent street demonstrations. His arguments against Anglo-Iranian were bolstered by both Venezuela and Saudi Arabia signing deals that gave them 50/50 profit splits with the oil companies working in those countries. In June, Iranian officials seized the company's offices in Tehran and Abadan. The British staff evacuated on a cruiser, carrying off their collections of Persian rugs. When the company's Iranian employees stormed the offices, they found evidence that many Iranian politicians benefited from Anglo-Iranian's largesse.

Both sides wore out a stable of U.S. statesmen trying to broker a deal. The best known of these was Averell Harriman, the tycoon turned diplomat, who was sent by President Harry Truman to work out a solution. Harriman was completely frustrated. Mossadegh would lie in bed in pink pajamas and a camel hair coat, resisting going where the diplomats tried to take him. Sometimes he didn't seem to have any interest in a solution. "You do not know how evil they are," he said of the British to Harriman. "They sully everything they touch." Other times he appeared to be open to serious talks. For instance, he offered full and fair negotiations on the company's claims to a senior British envoy, Sir Richard Stokes. When Stokes cabled London for permission to pursue what appeared to be an opening he was told "no further concessions."

Britain imposed an embargo and economic sanctions. A flotilla of British warships patrolled the Gulf off Iran, and the British debated landing a military force. In 1952, they seized a tanker called the Mary Rose that had loaded Iranian crude. At first the Americans were furious at the British. "Never had so few lost so much so stupidly and so fast," wrote Dean Acheson.

Then turmoil descended on Iran. Mossadegh resigned after a fainting spell in the Shah's office and was replaced by a pro-British politician named Ahmad Qavam, triggering waves of street protests. The military fired on protesters, leaving many dead. After Dwight Eisenhower's election in 1952, Washington shifted its focus to worry that the chaos in Tehran or a foolish British military would usher in a communist regime, playing into Moscow's hands. British intelligence stoked these fears.

Eisenhower was eventually convinced by the British and his own intelligence that the fears were well-founded and that working with Mossadegh was hopeless. The C.I.A. and British intelligence planned to overthrow him, and replace him with the Shah. "Operation Ajax," as it was known in the United States, or "Operation Boot" in Britain, was set in motion in August 1953. A first coup attempt on August 15 failed. A few days later a second coup succeeded. Iranians, as well as some western scholars, believe that by diverting the course of Iranian history away from the democratically chosen Mossadegh and toward the autocratic Shah, the U.S.- and British-inspired coup sowed the seeds of the Islamic Revolution a quarter of a century later.

And on top of that, Anglo-Iranian would never regain its old status. A new arrangement gave the Iranians half of the oil revenue, and Anglo-Iranian was forced to divvy up the rest with American companies and its rival, Shell. Still, discoveries in Libya, Abu Dhabi, and elsewhere helped the company to increase its production to about 3.8 million barrels per day by 1970 — about what it is now.

● ● ●

Within a few years of the Iranian coup, a new and irresistible wave of nationalizations deprived BP of almost all of the low cost Middle Eastern crude that had been its foundation. In 1971 BP pumped more than 4 million barrels per day of crude from its own wells, mostly in the Middle East. By 1976 its equity production had dwindled to just 460,000 barrels per day as country after country, including Muammar Qaddafi's Libya, Kuwait, and Qatar, took over their country's oil fields. BP had to buy almost all of the crude to put through its world distribution system at market prices. Even the Shah demanded and received such control at a meeting in St. Moritz, Switzerland in 1973.

BP had fallen far. But the company was already on the way to a solution: finding and recovering difficult oil with sophisticated technology, and moving into North America. BP had long been skeptical about finding much oil in Britain and in the North Sea, but the discovery by what are now Shell and ExxonMobil of a giant gas field called Groningen, off the Netherlands, began to change attitudes. BP was favored by the British government for the best leases. In 1965, it became the first company to discover oil, or at least gas, in British waters, hitting a field called West Sole. Weather and big waves made the North Sea dangerous. In an early precursor of the Gulf of Mexico disaster, the rig that made the find, a converted barge called the Sea Gem, collapsed in December 1965. Thirteen of 32 crew members died.

West Sole was drilled in about 80 feet of water, not a huge challenge. BP was already familiar with such depths from work in Abu Dhabi. For deeper forays BP and other companies began ordering drilling rigs called semi-submersibles. These were early versions of vessels like the Deepwater Horizon. Compared to the relatively small rigs of the past, these were enormous. BP's first semi-submersible, called the Sea Quest, was 320 feet high and weighed 15,000 tons. The triangular-shaped platform had three legs, to which flotation chambers were attached. When in use, much of the rig was submerged below the rough surface of the water, making the platform more stable. In 1970, the Sea Quest found the Forties Field, the first North Sea giant with about 4 billion barrels nearly 110 miles offshore from Aberdeen in Scotland. Producing the oil, which was below the seabed in 400 feet of water, presented as big a challenge to the company as a field like Thunder Horse did in the late 1990s. Production platforms for the Forties were built on piles thrust 300 feet into the seabed to withstand 90-foot waves and 130-mile-per-hour winds.

Meanwhile, Britain's grim financial situation forced the government, which held over two-thirds of BP's shares, to begin unloading its stake, beginning with what was known as "the sale of the century" in 1976. But an even bigger sale was to come later. Margaret Thatcher's government sold the remaining state shares in BP in 1987. The timing could hardly have been worse. Shortly after the announcement of the privatization with great fanfare, world stock markets took one of their deepest dives ever on October 19. Seeing a bargain, the Kuwaiti government started snapping up BP shares in what seemed like an effort to take control. The regulators forced the Kuwaitis to pare back their position to 10 percent.

BP also began developing another huge frontier region, Alaska. Geologists thought the terrain in Alaska resembled that of Iran, and BP had been looking there since the early 1960s. The first area where BP focused, the foothills of the Brooks Range, proved a dud. But BP kept adjusting. In a piece of outstanding exploration savvy, a BP geologist, Jim Spence, figured out not only that Prudhoe Bay was an outstanding prospect, but that the most oil might be found in acreage on the peripheries of the field, which would go cheaper in lease auctions. In the first Prudhoe Bay auction in 1965, BP was outbid by an American consortium consisting of Atlantic Richfield Corp. and Humble Oil for what appeared to be the choicest acreage, but the British company managed to pick up 81,000 acres at an average price of $17.80.

Tired of drilling dry holes, BP came close to giving up. It closed the office in Los Angeles responsible for Alaska and put out inquiries to sell its leases. But when Atlantic Richfield found oil in 1967 with a rig relinquished by BP, the British company found itself still holding the best leases. BP struck oil in Prudhoe Bay in 1969 and later announced its share of the field had five billion barrels. It was the largest field ever discovered in the U.S. Thanks to the shrewdness of its explorers and the size of the field, BP's finding costs were just 30 cents a barrel, comparable to the dirt cheap Middle East.

Daniel Yergin, in *The Prize,* notes that the North Sea and the North Slope of Alaska had much in common. Exploiting their resources required a new generation of technology. "Though their reserves were in very difficult places, physically, they were not in unstable places, politically," he says. Those big discoveries helped make BP the standout explorer in the 1960s, finding 31 billion barrels from 1963 to 1970—double the tally of the closest competitor, Standard Oil of New Jersey (now ExxonMobil).

BP encountered obstacles on the North Slope, though of a different sort than they encountered in the Middle East. The oil was being produced in the northernmost reaches of Alaska, but wasn't worth a dime unless is could be brought 800 miles south to Valdez, a port city near Anchorage, where it would be loaded onto supertankers and transported to California. BP and its partners, ExxonMobil and ARCO, wanted to build a pipeline the length of the state. They didn't foresee the opposition they would face. Native Americans objected to its route going through their land, as did environmentalists, who argued that it would block caribou migrations and otherwise harm wildlife and the fragile arctic ecosystem. Environmental groups succeeded in blocking the pipeline in Federal court in 1970. Tens of millions of dollars worth of pipes and construction equipment bought for the project in 1968 lay idle for five years on the banks of the Yukon River until Congress gave a green light in the wake of the oil embargo following the 1973 Arab-Israeli war.

Without the Trans Alaska pipeline the 1989 Exxon Valdez spill, a black mark for the oil industry for two decades afterward, would never have occurred. John Browne, who would later become one of BP's most influential CEOs, recalls flying over the grounded tanker on the day it happened. His conclusion: This was a gift to environmental groups opposed to exploitation of oil in sensitive areas. "The industry was now measured by its weakest member, the one with the worst reputation," he writes. "That oil company was now Exxon." Twenty years later, the tables were turned and ExxonMobil had found a kind of redemption. After the Deepwater Horizon, BP was the weak link and ExxonMobil the example that others, including BP, wanted to emulate.

BP's activity in the Gulf of Mexico is a direct extension of that swashbuckling legacy, a combination of shrewd study of the geology and an adventuresome spirit. Strangely, when put under stress, as it has been following the Macondo debacle, BP has repeatedly displayed a lack of savvy about host country politics and a tendency to say the wrong thing, reminiscent of what caused it so much trouble in mid-twentieth-century Iran.

Chapter 4

The Big Kahuna of the Gulf

The Gulf of Mexico blowout on April 20 came as a big shock for Dave Rainey. Up to that moment, the well, known as Macondo, hadn't been a big worry for the head of BP's Gulf of Mexico exploration team. Rainey had been pleased when earlier in April he received word that the well team had found oil. BP was even preparing a press release announcing the find. It was a modest, 50-million-barrel discovery, but the plan was to tie Macondo to an old platform about 20 miles away called Pompano. Reusing a platform would make the oil more profitable and would help reduce BP's environmental footprint, Rainey said. He called Macondo "infrastructure-led exploration"—boring stuff compared to the hunts for giant fields that are BP explorers' lifeblood.

Rainey knew the well had been tricky. There had been at least one gas incident, called a "kick," and some fracturing in the rock wall of the well. But BP's drillers didn't think it was difficult enough to abandon. And they had completed it despite the problems. What was unusual was for a completed well to blow up. Usually if there are problems, they occur as the drillers are inching their way down through the rocks, Rainey said.

That night changed everything for Rainey and his team. The next day he was representing BP at a press conference in New Orleans. Now, instead of hunting for oil, he was being transferred to BP's new Gulf recovery unit, called the Gulf Coast Restoration Organization. He was now leading the science side of the effort, handing out research grants to institutions, such as Louisiana State University and the Florida Institute of Oceanography, to study the effects of the oil spill. The moratorium on offshore drilling in the United States meant his old exploration team couldn't drill for new oil or develop existing finds. Instead, in the months after Macondo, they worked on the relief wells snaking down into the Gulf seabed to shut off the flow of oil. The impact of the Macondo disaster is not limited to just the Gulf of Mexico. Key executives from other operations around the world were called to Houston to help manage the mess, in some cases disrupting their own operations. Exploration drilling off Libya, to mention one case, was delayed for months. In the fall of 2010, production at the showcase Thunder Horse field was down sharply by 50,000 barrels per day because the company was unable to drill additional wells.

The Gulf of Mexico disaster has been particularly devastating for BP's Houston employees because, right up to the blowout, the GOM, as it is known, was BP's pride and joy. The company has been the unquestioned leader in the industry's move out into the deep water of the Gulf of Mexico, touting big recent discoveries, the most production, the most leases, a track record of innovation, and a vision of the future. Until April 2010, BP's casually dressed Houston employees had a cheerful swagger.

After the blowout, the atmosphere became tense and grim. There were humorous moments though. Whenever CEO Tony Hayward or other BP executives gave a press conference at the Houston headquarters, vultures could be seen circling outside the window, apparently enjoying the updrafts created by BP's high-rise building, known as Westlake 4.

The explorers liked to hang out in a big dark, windowless room called the hive on the third floor of their building. They used the hive for viewing three-dimensional seismic images and debating which bits of seabed to target for new drilling. Once the blowout occurred, the room was transformed into part of the operation center for the long fight to shut down the runaway well. Tables of food and coffee were set up outside in the corridors. Instead of being a gathering place for scientists pondering the meaning of seismic images and trying to imagine what happened tens of millions of years ago, the hive became the home of technicians monitoring the eerie movements of undersea robots around the spewing well on an array of video screens. Inglis, the E&P chief who only a year earlier had led an exuberant tour of the Thunder Horse platform, was silent in May 2010, as he oversaw the maddeningly long shut down effort.

● ● ●

BP began its foray into the deep water of the Gulf of Mexico more than 20 years earlier, before the Amoco acquisition and well before John Browne became CEO. Offshore drilling had been underway in the shallow waters of the Gulf for decades, and the area was well-picked over, with around 40 billion barrels discovered. BP's U.S. explorers were rethinking their strategy and focusing on big fields—what they called "elephants." Oil fields with more than 500 million barrels accounted for only one percent of all fields discovered, but they held 75 percent of the reserves. There had been plenty of those found in the shallow waters of the bayous and continental shelf, and they suspected there were more lurking further out in the Gulf, in waters more than 1,000 feet deep. Only a small number of discoveries had come in deep water by 1985, totaling less than 150 million barrels.

BP gained a small presence in the Gulf through its acquisition of Standard Oil of Ohio in the 1980s. That opened a window for its global explorers. They studied the region and zeroed in on some acreage held by Shell, which turned down an early BP approach to joint venture. Later, after Shell made a huge investment acquiring leases in the Chukchi Sea off Alaska, it allowed BP a minority stake in what turned out to be a giant field called Mars, in return for BP's funding a hefty share of the costs. A BP executive, who was involved at the time, said that the company had already scoped out Shell's property and liked what it saw. BP also wanted to partner with Shell, a world-class company. The deal looked like an ideal route for BP to learn about the Gulf of Mexico, and in many ways it was.

Shell executives kick themselves for letting BP in, a move that eventually caused them to cede their early lead in the deep water. In the following years their Gulf effort lost momentum, while BP's production surged. However, it wasn't a simple story. Jazzed up by Mars, found in 1988, and other discoveries, BP and Shell went on a drilling binge trying to replicate the big hit. With ExxonMobil, BP made one score called Diana. But it also drilled a costly series of dry holes called Sycamore, Tobruk, and Blue Ridge. Such wells now cost up to $200 million. Mars and other recent finds such as Ursa had been discovered by drilling "bright spots" that looked like oil on seismic surveys, maps generated by bouncing sound waves off the rocks below the earth's surface, but that approach turned out to be a false lead.

The basic tool that offshore explorers use to see below the surface of the earth are images of the subsurface produced by sound waves fired from boats and then recorded as they bounce back off structures deep in the earth. The reams of data generated are then processed into maps that give explorers a look at what is underground. Still, interpreting the maps requires some judgment and guesswork, so drilling is the only way to confirm their hunches.

Rainey arrived in Houston from Alaska in 1991 on the day BP came up empty on Sycamore. He recalls an atmosphere of gloom about the Gulf. The region was dubbed the "Dead Sea" in the Houston press. Other companies gave up, thinking the area was played out and too expensive. Cindy Yeilding, who is now the chief Gulf explorer, remembers being fearful that BP's Gulf group, too, would get the chop.

Instead, BP's brain trust, including Browne, who was head of exploration and production at the time, looked at what is called the "creaming curve" of the Gulf, a simple graph in which the size of each discovery is plotted against time. What they saw intrigued them. The finds in deeper water were growing in size, not leveling off. That's the classic pattern of an oil play with legs, not one that is mature. Their conclusion: The Gulf of Mexico might have very difficult geology to interpret, but it also had a world-class future. In fact, 18 billion barrels have now been found in the deep water, Rainey figures, and BP thinks that may be less than half of what's there.

Instead of firing its explorers, BP management told them to go back to the drawing boards and come up with a new plan of attack. It was a turning point for the company.

BP is good at applying what it has learned in other parts of the world to new regions and bringing in explorers with a global perspective to help local experts, such as the Gulf team. BP's Gulf explorers gave up drilling what looked like easy wins but turned out to be huge money wasters and went back to basic petroleum geology.

As they do in promising regions around the world, the geologists tried to think through what had happened to the rocks below the sea floor over tens of millions of years. They tried to figure out where in the Gulf large amounts of oil, which is formed from the remnants of organisms that died more than 100 million years ago, might have migrated up through the earth's crust and then become trapped. An oil field is like an overturned bathtub filled with sponge. Over millions of years, the oil, when heated up in the earth's crust, flows up from the original source rocks and, in fortuitous circumstances, fills layers of porous sandstone formed from sediment laid down by ancient rivers or other action. Because the tub is lined with impermeable shale or salt, the oil can't escape. To be a successful explorer, "You have to learn to think like an oil molecule," Rainey says.

Cindy Yeilding, a bubbly, blonde geologist, was key to the rethink. Whenever she could escape from BP's Houston headquarters, she'd travel to Quebec or Arkansas or France, places where time had exposed rocks called turbidites that were similar to those below the Gulf sea floor. These rocks are formed from the debris of undersea landslides and form the spongy sandstones that hold Gulf oil. One veteran explorer, Neil Piggott, even went 2,000 feet down in the Gulf in a submarine to get a firsthand look at seeps of oil and gas bleeding out of the sea bottom. There in the inky darkness he saw masses of bacteria feeding on the oil, and bizarre, 30-foot tube worms that eat the bacteria. The seeps were hard evidence that further out in the Gulf there was more oil to find. They are also a reminder that oil is naturally part of the ecology of the Gulf.

Advances in drilling technology gave the explorers added firepower. Major oil companies like BP hire contractors, such as Transocean Ltd. and Diamond Offshore Drilling Co., who specialize in drilling the actual well. Transocean, the largest offshore drilling company, has more than 275 drilling rigs and drill-ships. The drillers had told BP and other oil companies that if the oil companies would commit to long-term leases, the drillers would build powerful, fifth generation rigs capable of extending the early 1990s drilling range from 5,000 feet of water and 20,000 feet of rock, to 10,000 feet and 30,000 feet or even more.

BP contracted for the exclusive use of four new rigs, including Transocean's Deepwater Horizon. With the added seismic power that opened up a whole new world to the explorers, "We saw signs that there were big structures down there, but they were out of range," Rainey said.

By the late 1990s, BP's explorers had drawn up a series of maps of the Gulf terrain, and they had worked up a list of the most promising prospects for finding big fields. They had also made big changes in their Gulf lease positions. Through swaps and bidding at the semi-annual lease auctions the U.S. government holds in New Orleans, BP accumulated leases over areas that their rethink told them had the most promising prospects. Yeilding called it a "land grab." By late 2010, BP was the largest holder of Gulf leases, with about 500.

The Gulf explorers soon identified the Mississippi Canyon area as a place where a giant field might be lurking. But, Yeilding said, they had reason to be wary. BP simplifies exploration decisions down to a three-light traffic signal model. Is there a source for oil nearby? Is there a rock seal to trap it? Are the rocks that form the potential reservoir sufficiently porous for the oil to flow out? The explorers were confident that oil had flowed into the trap and that there was a seal to lock it in, but they worried about the reservoir. Would the rocks bearing the oil be so deep and exposed to such high temperatures that they would be like concrete and unable to yield up their treasure?

Adding to their angst, a well that they spudded nearby on a less promising prospect in 1997 was unsuccessful. Exploration wells are extremely expensive, costing up to $200 million, and failed wells are morale killers if not a threat to jobs. "Every explorer is physically upset when you drill a dry hole," Rainey said.

Despite misgivings, they began a well known as MC 911-1, in January 1999. It proved a huge success, hitting more than 500 feet of oil-bearing rock in three different zones. The field, now named Thunder Horse, may hold as much as a billion barrels of recoverable oil and gas. It's the third largest oil field in the United States, and the biggest in the Gulf.

For Cindy Yeilding, April 22, 1999, was a big night. That is when the drilling rig on Thunder Horse first struck oil. The actual well site was 150 miles southeast of New Orleans, in the Gulf of Mexico, in 6000 feet of water. Yeilding had been monitoring a feed from the rig on a computer at her home. Because her husband works for another oil company, when news of the discovery came through she went out in the garage, where she spent most of the night on the phone with her team.

BP also made two other big discoveries around the same time. In the fanciful language of the Gulf they were called Atlantis and Mad Dog. Mad Dog was on a lease that partly came with the Amoco purchase. All told, BP participates in more than 20 producing fields in the deep water of the Gulf and is the operator on at least eight. BP properties stretch across the water in a wide band that starts with a cluster of fields east of New Orleans and finishes about 500 miles westward toward the Mexican border with Texas.

Finding oil in the deep water is challenging enough; getting it out represents another huge task. Nine years elapsed between the first discovery and the start of production on Thunder Horse. Often projects that start under a CEO or an area manager only start to pay off after she or he is gone. At Thunder Horse, BP planned to drill 33 wells, some of them for water injection, to hook up to a single production rig. With those ambitious plans, the company wanted a rig that could keep drilling wells after production. They ordered up a platform known as a PDQ for "production, drilling, quarters."

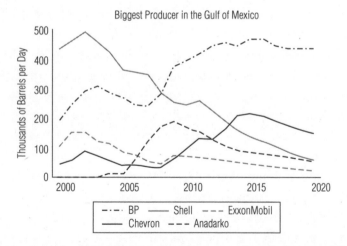

BP's commitment to the Gulf of Mexico after other companies gave it up as a "dead sea" allowed the company to become the dominant player in the deep water of the Gulf. *Source:* Wood Mackenzie/BP (May 2009).

The oil wells you find on a field like Thunder Horse have evolved a long way from the nodding donkeys or other contraptions of popular lore. Modern day drilling rigs are capable of hitting small targets miles away from the platform. The wells, started from drilling centers on the bottom, snake out not only tens of thousands of feet into the earth but miles away from the production unit. They can be steered precisely so as to hit multiple sweet spots in an oil-bearing formation. In this way a single platform can be used to drain a sizeable region. The oil reservoirs of Thunder Horse, for instance, lie buried under nine contiguous lease blocks, each covering nine square miles. And the wells are tremendously productive—up to 55,000 barrels per day in the case of some at Thunder Horse.

When you fly out to Thunder Horse on a helicopter, it's not immediately clear how big it is. The vast, empty sea around it makes it look small. But when you clamber around this hulking monster that floats on four red-painted columns you begin to appreciate how huge it is. The deck is a gigantic 149 by 122 yards. The hull alone weighs more than 60,000 tons and was made in South Korea and shipped aboard a specially modified vessel. Modules for housing the crew and other uses weigh another 20,000 tons.

Building deepwater oil fields is a huge technological challenge, testing the frontiers the way a space mission did in the 1960s or a sailing ship voyage did in the sixteenth century. Once something goes wrong you are in deep trouble—no pun intended. The oil and gas are under explosive pressure, and the platforms can be a hundred or more miles away from shore and rescue.

Much of the equipment for handling the oil is installed on the sea bottom more than a mile below the surface where no human can go. Whatever work that needs to be done on the bottom is performed by underwater robots guided by "pilots" above using joysticks like those employed in video games. The equipment is painted yellow so it stands out in the darkness in the headlights of the robots floating in the depths. Seventy new sub-sea products, from stacks of valves called Christmas trees to special pipes strong enough and flexible enough to carry the oil a mile to the surface and withstand the strong Loop currents, had to be created just for Thunder Horse to deal with fluids flowing at searing temperatures of up to 275 degrees and explosive pressures of 17,400 pounds per square inch.

With Thunder Horse, BP flirted with disaster of Macondo-like proportions. In 2005, Hurricane Dennis passed, leaving Thunder Horse tilting to one side, nearly sinking, thanks to faults in the ballast system that let in water. A year of costly repairs followed. Then in 2006 defective welds were found on some of the subsea oil handling equipment, necessitating another round of delays and very expensive fixes. Massive pieces of metal equipment had to be brought to the surface, re-welded, and then fitted back into place.

Part of the problem was that Thunder Horse was cutting edge, a foray into the unknown. But there is also a sense around the industry that BP made things more complicated than they needed to be, and that in general it doesn't execute projects very well. Hayward himself used to say that BP was not always up to snuff at building projects. In early 2010, he announced an effort to standardize and centralize such work on the lines of ExxonMobil. "When BP is good, it is fantastic," he told *Horizon*, the in-house magazine, in 2007. "Unfortunately, when we are bad, we are very poor. . . ."

Thunder Horse is now one of BP's stalwarts despite the snafus. In 2009 it was producing around its plateau of 300,000 barrels per day of oil and gas, making it the second most prolific field in the United States after Prudhoe Bay. And its oil is among the most profitable in BP's portfolio, according to Inglis. It earns the company an estimated $20 per barrel, roughly three times what BP makes on a barrel in Russia, another stronghold, estimates Fadel Gheit, an analyst at Oppenheimer & Co. in New York.

Until the Deepwater Horizon accident, Washington had good reason to view BP's Gulf activities as a big plus for U.S. energy security interests rather than a threat to the well-being of the region. After all, Thunder Horse alone was producing oil worth about $17 million a day or around $6.4 billion a year at a price of $70 per barrel, a lot of which would go to the government. BP's projects including Thunder Horse and Atlantis contributed a large chunk of the 7 percent growth in production the United States achieved in 2009, reversing an 18-year decline. About one-third of total U.S. oil output—around 5.3 million barrels per day—comes from the Gulf of Mexico. Deep water has kept the Gulf, which looked dead two decades ago, a viable producing region and the raison d'être for a thriving, global industry.

In 2009, BP produced about 440 thousand barrels per day of oil and gas from the Gulf of Mexico, about 11 percent of its output. Even after the Macondo debacle, BP believes it will become even more of a deepwater company in the future, unless it is barred from doing so

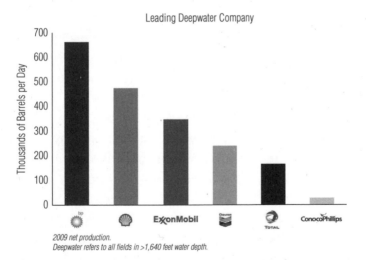

Through its production in the Gulf of Mexico and offshore Angola, BP is now the world's leading deepwater company. The deep water is also likely to play an even bigger role in BP's future.
Source: Wood Mackenzie (March 2010).

by the United States or other countries. It's already the world's leading deepwater producer, obtaining about 18 percent of its production from oil and gas produced in challenging water depths not only in the GOM but off Angola and, in the future, off the coasts of Egypt, Libya, and Brazil. With the company putting simpler onshore and shallow water fields on the block to help pay the costs of cleaning up the Gulf of Mexico and legal claims, its dependence on deep water is likely to accelerate, assuming the company gets back on track.

● ● ●

What's surprising given BP's commitment to deepwater drilling is how ill-prepared it was to deal with a blowout on the sea bottom. While plans for cleaning up a mess on the surface were well-developed, the company could do little more than improvise its way to a solution to the oil flowing from the stricken well a mile below the surface. More than once CEO Tony Hayward admitted that BP had been unprepared. "There is an enormous amount of learning going on here, because we are doing it for real for the first time," he said in May 2010, referring to the frustratingly slow efforts to cap the well and stop the flow of oil.

The deepwater push has created good jobs. Some 7,000 of BP's 23,000 U.S. employees work in the Houston area, many in a suburban office park just off the Katy Freeway in what is known as the Energy Corridor. There BP employs large teams of engineers, geologists, and computer scientists. "These are highly compensated people; it's no longer Jim Bob and Billy Rae with a pickup truck," says J. Robinson West, Chairman of Washington, D.C.-based consultants PFC Energy.

To keep hitting home runs like Mars and Thunder Horse in the Gulf, a company needs to keep testing the limits of physical technology and geological time. The game keeps changing in the Gulf, and the companies that are most successful are those that anticipate the changes and are early to exploit them. The first big discoveries in the deep-water Gulf were in the East. The oil-bearing rocks were from relatively recent geological periods, about 14 million years ago, called the Pliocene and Miocene.

Fields such as Mars and Ursa were also mostly outside the shadows of the salt domes that obscure much of the oil in the Gulf. When ancient seas were baked away more than a hundred million years ago, they left vast layers of salt. Later, when sediment came down the predecessors of the Mississippi River, it created the sandstones that now contain oil and gas. The weight of these rocks squeezed the salt upwards into canopies that overhang the salt like beach umbrellas. Vast expanses of salt, thousands of feet thick, now hide much of the oil and gas. Because salt distorts seismic waves, it makes it very hard for explorers to see what is under it. BP executives are fond of saying that trying to see what is under salt is like looking through a frosted glass door to see who is in the shower. Salt also makes drilling more risky by concealing sudden pressure changes.

BP's explorers have been among those in the forefront of solving the problems created by these salt formations that cover much of the oil and gas accumulations, not only in the Gulf, but in other deepwater regions such as Brazil. While many companies tailored their exploration so as to skirt the salt, BP's explorers spent $100 million in the early part of the twenty-first century on new techniques for looking through the stuff.

To try to get accurate pictures, BP's scientists have done everything—from placing dozens of sound receptors on the sea floor and then picking them all up again—to modifying the specialized ships that criss-cross the waters over likely oil deposits and pinging them with air guns. A key innovation is to tow streams of seismic sensors, as long as four miles, behind boats that fire off air guns, so as to obtain pictures of the subsurface from different angles. Then the company puts supercomputers to work crunching the resulting data into maps that help pinpoint where to drill. "We stopped being afraid of the salt," says Cindy Yeilding. "In fact, salt has become an integral part of our exploration strategy."

Drilling in a mile or more of water and 30,000 feet into the ground may seem hugely risky, but in some respects the oil companies have cut the risk through technology. Because wells are so expensive, the explorers spend years studying prospects before drilling into them. Seismic technology, married to computer software, can produce three-dimensional models of an oil field five miles below the sea floor, giving the exploration team a good idea of not only where to drill to find oil but, later, how best to locate the wells so as to most efficiently drain the reserves.

That sort of model building is one of the key advances that made it possible for BP and other companies to operate under conditions that not long ago would have been unthinkable. Bigger, more powerful drilling rigs are another essential development. Not long ago, drilling a 25,000-foot well would have taken eons because the rigs lacked not only the power but the accuracy of today's behemoths. Even Thunder Horse required six months to complete—from January 1, 1999, to the fourth of July. Finally, the technology for actually producing the oil has also made huge strides. It's possible to build something to deal with just about any conditions.

Yeilding considers Mars a stage one discovery—a phase of Gulf exploration that ran from the mid-1980s to mid-1990s and found about 9 billion barrels. She puts Thunder Horse in the second stage of deepwater drilling into deeper and older rock, which has found about 6 billion barrels. The explorers call Thunder Horse a turtle because, with a flat bottom and curved top, it looks like one of the beasts.

Two other big second stage finds, Atlantis and Mad Dog, are what are called "fold belt" plays. These fields are found more than a hundred miles from shore in the Gulf where a layer of sedimentary rock extending out from the land mass meets what is called the abyssal plain, the bottom of the sea. Up to that point, the rock is cushioned by a layer of salt that lubricates its movement. But the salt runs out at the abyssal plain leading to folds, which serve as traps for oil.

Busy with Thunder Horse in the early twenty-first century, BP largely sat tight and watched the industry gradually move into what may be a new stage and an older geological zone called the Paleogene or Lower Tertiary, where the reservoir rocks date back 50 million years. Thunder Horse is thought to be from the Miocene period of about 14 million years ago.

The Gulf is a series of plays, and the trick is to keep thinking of new ones that might produce oil rather than sticking with a strategy that has already produced its best finds. Pressed by Inglis and Hayward about standing pat, the Gulf explorers responded with a 2005 memo that said in their view the industry was skirting around the edges of the ancient Gulf salt deposits where the reservoirs were relatively small and the oil heavy and difficult to extract. The BP paper, Rainey says, argued "we need to move further North and West under the salt to look for better fluids and better reservoirs."

BP's approach began paying dividends when the Deepwater Horizon, which worked exclusively for BP throughout its existence, discovered the huge Paleogene field called Kaskida in 2006. It may have four to six billion barrels of oil in place. Experts think these Paleogene fields may hold the largest amount of oil in the Gulf. The reservoirs found so far have been very large. Lauren B. Segal, who was in charge of drilling the wells to figure out just how much oil was in Kaskida, said the field had 800 feet of oil-bearing rocks, a very large amount. The question is whether the oil companies will figure out how to get the oil out economically. The oil in these fields tends to be heavier and to produce less per well—a worry given the high cost of drilling in such places.

In the fall of 2009 the ill-fated Deepwater Horizon had another, even bigger triumph, when it struck oil in a field called Tiber, in what is called the Keathley Canyon. Tiber is 250 miles southeast of Houston in water about 4,000 feet deep. At 35,055 feet in total, the Tiber well may be the deepest well ever drilled. To put the depth into perspective, the well is substantially longer than Mount Everest is tall. In fact, its length is comparable to the cruising altitude of a jetliner. Yet at that distance, the oil companies manage to hit relatively small targets through a mile of water and several miles of rock and salt. Michael Daly, BP's chief of exploration, said Tiber was "even better" than Kaskida. Inglis at the time said Tiber and Kaskida "support the continuing growth of our deepwater Gulf of Mexico business into the second half of the next decade."

What is ironic is that the well that has brought BP to its knees was far from its most ambitious. The company was scoping out a relatively small trove of oil—perhaps 50 million barrels—that could be produced by a nearby platform called Pompano, an early field whose production has been in decline. This was a peanut project compared to Thunder Horse or Tiber, but such "infrastructure-led exploration" can be lucrative because the company doesn't need to spend much money on new platforms and other equipment to produce the oil. "This is something that, with any kind of reasonable practices, should have been able to be drilled without a problem," said James Hackett, CEO of Anadarko Petroleum Corp. and BP's 25 percent partner on Macondo, in an interview at Houston's River Oaks Country Club. Hackett also did not think he had any reason to doubt BP's capabilities.

The lesson here is that when you actually go to drill the result may turn out to be quite different from what the explorers theorize. While the geologists with Ph.D.s who seek out the oil with technology and computers usually aren't afraid of getting their hands dirty, they are often from vastly different backgrounds than the workers who actually live on the rig, drilling down for the oil.

Rig work is one of the last great opportunities for the undereducated American or, for that matter, Briton. A man—and they are almost all men—with only a high school diploma or even a GED can start as a roughneck, painting rusty patches and mopping decks, and earn $50,000 a year or more for work that allows him as many days off as he works. That doesn't make it part-time, however. He'll work 12-hour shifts, seven days a week, for three weeks straight. That's an

84-hour work week in sweltering heat or high winds or driving rain, wearing goggles, steel-toed boots, and helmets no matter the weather. He spends much of his day in safety meetings and practicing drills.

With long hours and hard, physical work, the people on the rig develop a fraternal bond. When you arrive as a new guy, you're immediately given a nickname—something like "dog" or "bone-head" or "gant." "You don't really know where they come from," says Phil Tobey, who worked his way up from roustabout to rig manager over a 30-year career at Diamond Offshore Drilling. Someone who's short might be called "pub joint" after a short drill pipe. A "worm" or "green-hand" is a new guy to the job. The crew is likely to give that guy a green hard hat so they can spot him and watch out for him until he becomes more seasoned.

That's because there's constant danger when you're offshore. Just getting to work is an adventure. Rig workers are transported either by helicopter from Houma, Louisiana, or by boat from Port Fourchon. The helicopter lands directly on the platform. From a boat, you're lifted by crane onto the rig using a contraption called a Billy Pugh basket, a circular rubber ring with net around it that looks like an upside down ice cream cone. You throw your bag in the middle of the net, and stand on the edge of the ring clinging to the netting while you're hauled up 100 feet or so to the platform. In calm weather it usually goes well, but in wind and rough seas, it's not hard to fall, or to be slammed against the side of the rig or down onto the deck of the rising and falling transport boat. Plaintiff's lawyers in Houston and New Orleans have made careers out of the Billy Pugh basket.

A semi-submersible rig such as the Deepwater Horizon sits on giant pontoons in the water that fill with water when the rig reaches the drill site in order to partially submerge. Sitting deep in the water makes the platform much more stable. The pontoons have thrusters in them that are tied to satellite global positioning devices in order to keep the rig in place above the well. They also have pumps inside that must constantly readjust their ballast to ensure the rig remains upright.

The pumps and thrusters emit a constant hum throughout the ship. Under the law, the floating rig is a ship, with a licensed captain and crew capable of running a ship and drilling a well.

Rigs like Deepwater Horizon are the class of the industry, and they have evolved a long way from the more basic contraptions that do drilling in shallower waters. For one thing everything is computerized, much is automated, and the rigs are a lot more comfortable. The driller sits in an air-conditioned cab watching consoles. The only thing unchanged: There is usually an empty coffee can nearby to be used as a spittoon.

The work on the rig is all about pressure. Working that deep underwater, and that far under the earth's crust, means dealing with pressures equivalent to having about 650 feet of steel bricks piled on top of you. The pressure would kill anyone who went down there. Drillers, above all, must maintain enough pressure on top of the oil and gas that want to surge to the surface and escape once free from the confines of the depths of the earth. They put drilling fluid, or mud, down the hole as they cut into the earth, the only barrier against the surging hydrocarbons below. And they monitor it constantly with gauges that measure the pressure.

The pressure comes from elsewhere as well. There are schedules and goals. This well needs to get done so we can move onto the next. There are cost pressures—a drilling rig alone leases for half a million dollars a day, and that doesn't include the costs of the mud, or the pipes, or the caterer who is making the food for the guy with the GED from Mississippi.

● ● ●

While former BP executives say the company wasn't prone to taking excessive risks or cutting corners, they concede that the Macondo well was very late and, therefore, way over budget. That is the time, if ever, that drillers and other employees might be tempted to take liberties with established practices.

The top dog in BP exploration is Michael Daly, a lanky, affable Irishman, who is based in London. Daly survived Macondo and retained his post on the new top team Dudley announced on Sept. 29, 2010. Daly is on the hook to come up with at least 500,000 barrels of new reserves per year, and has been doing better than that, averaging around 800 million. For eight years, through 2008, BP led its peers among the majors in what is known as organic reserve replacement—additions to its reserve base that don't include any oil picked up through mergers.

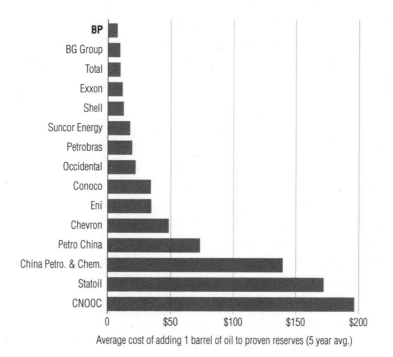

Average cost of adding 1 barrel of oil to proven reserves (5 year avg.)

BP's success in finding massive fields means the company's costs per barrel discovered are lower than its competitors'. That sort of track record has led BP to evolve in a different way than other majors such as ExxonMobil and Shell. It is unique as an exploration-led major. "It never felt like an engineering company," says Jim Farnsworth, a former exploration chief. "It was unique in being an exploration-led super-major. Exploration performance was used as an example to the rest of the organization."
Source: Bloomberg News, Seth Myers.

Daly gathers his 15 or so chief lieutenants from around the world four times a year, usually in Houston or London, to decide where to spend money next. One meeting, in July 2009, was at a hotel in Britain's Hampshire County. The goal was to back the best ideas from around the globe, rather than simply spread the $600 million to $1 billion BP has to spend on exploration evenly among the various teams. The team proposing drilling a prospect puts their thinking down on a few pages setting out what they expect to find including the amount of oil and gas, the thickness of the reservoir, and the cost of drilling. According to one participant, the discussion can get quite tense, "because people are battling for projects they care about." BP's success rate on the 15 to 25 exploration wells it drills is about 60 percent.

Daly and other top explorers say the best people at finding oil aren't the usual corporate types. There's an element of art as well as science, says Yeilding. Good scientific knowledge and experience is paramount, but good explorers also need to have the insight "to make a leap," Daly says.

For instance, John Etgen, a Houston-based exploration scientist, looked at the work of BP crews trying to map winding gas fields off the Nile Delta in Egypt by zigzagging back and forth with their listening boats, and then came up with the idea of towing the streamers over the Gulf salt layers. That initiative, Daly says, led both to Tiber and a big new discovery around Mad Dog.

Even before the Macondo blowout BP explorers say they knew they had better not become too smug. About four years ago they drilled a well they were so excited about that they called it Big Kahuna. They found nothing. They had the geology completely wrong. "We try to stay humble," Rainey says. "Because when we don't, we get kicked in the behind." That mistake only cost them tens of millions. The mistakes on the Macondo well killed 11 people and came close to bringing down one of the world's largest companies.

Chapter 5

Money, Politics, and Bad Timing

I n Port Fourchon, the southernmost port in Louisiana perched on the end of Grand Isle, life revolves around oil rigs and fishing. This tiny town of Cajuns, canals, docks, and honky-tonks services 90 percent of the deepwater oil rigs and platforms in the Gulf and hosts the Louisiana Offshore Oil Port.

Those oil platforms produce 30 percent of U.S. oil and 10 percent of its natural gas, and the offshore industry accounted for as many as 400,000 jobs, and $70 billion in economic activity, according to IHS Global Insight. That includes the workers at offshore transport companies Edison Chouest and Hornbeck and the waiters and bartenders at Mes Amis who make burgers and serve beers to the locals.

The oil industry here and down the coast in Texas is both the anchor and the growth industry. It's got a long past, but with the expansion of deepwater drilling and the rise in prices, it's also the future. As technological advances make drilling more and more complex, and more lucrative, the oil towns around the Gulf, from Port Fourchon across to Houston, have boomed. Port Fourchon and Houma, Louisiana, a key logistics base for BP, throb with the activity of people and fuel moving to and from the massive factories floating out in the water. Houston, which boasts a Shell Plaza and gleaming blue glass towers hosting companies such as Schlumberger, Chevron, Devon Energy, and Marathon Oil, has become a Silicon Valley for the petroleum engineer. It's a place to make money and to make it big.

These jobs are precious to the locals who depend on them, and they're equally precious to the politicians who represent the region and win reelection when their constituents are happy. The politics of oil, however, is fraught in the United States. Liberals are often opposed to anything that benefits oil companies whom they paint as powerful corporate forces and reckless polluters. Conservatives support the lucrative industry that creates jobs and wealth. But when prices rise, the sides are muddied because nobody likes to pay more to fuel their cars and heat their homes.

In 2010, President Barack Obama stepped into this mire when he turned his back on liberal orthodoxy and advocated for expanding offshore drilling. At that moment, the move was seen as an artful political play that might help him win Republican support for his environmental agenda. It was also a victory for the oil industry, which had sought access to closed-off U.S. waters for decades. It turned out to be supremely bad timing for both. Within three weeks of Obama's March 31 announcement, the Deepwater Horizon exploded in the Gulf and both the presidency and the industry saw their hopes go up in flames.

● ● ●

Offshore drilling in the United States has been largely limited to the Western Gulf of Mexico and some parts of Alaska since 1981, when Congress prohibited new offshore leases elsewhere. The ban was the last of a flurry of environmental laws passed after a 1969 blowout on a shallow water offshore rig left 40 miles of beaches near Santa Barbara, California, blackened, sticky, and smelling of petroleum.

When the Exxon Valdez oil tanker ran aground, dumping its entire payload into Alaska's Prince William Sound in 1989, President George H.W. Bush reinforced the annual congressional moratorium with his own executive order. He, too, excluded the Western Gulf of Mexico, and so states from Texas to Mississippi, in whose coastal waters drilling is permitted, remained friendly to companies such as BP and Shell. Still, through the 1990s and the first part of this century, oil was cheap and plentiful, the Soviet bloc had collapsed, and the United States was at peace. Congress re-upped its ban on new oil exploration every year without a word. New sources of oil did not seem to be needed. The result is the United States stands out as one of the few countries in the world that prefers to leave what could be large deposits of oil and gas in the ground, while importing a high proportion of its consumption.

●●●

In the Spring of 2000, that began to change when electricity shortages in California led to rolling blackouts across the state as wholesale and consumer prices skyrocketed as much as tenfold. The price of crude oil rose from about $8 a barrel in December 1998 to more than $30 a barrel in November 2000.

President George W. Bush, the son of the president who put the offshore moratorium in place, entered office in January 2001 focused on boosting energy supplies in the United States. Just two weeks after he took office, Bush, an unsuccessful Texas wildcatter before he became governor, ordered his Vice President, Dick Cheney, to head up a task force that would outline an energy policy that would focus on developing domestic supplies.

The convergence of rising prices and two oilmen taking over the White House meant the already powerful industry gained new influence in Washington. It was their moment to try to loosen the tight controls the United States had placed on new exploration in hopes of finding new reservoirs in the politically stable and investor friendly United States.

Cheney, the former CEO of oil services giant Halliburton, the same company that was responsible for cementing BP's Macondo well, consulted in secret with oil companies and utilities while formulating his recommendations. The companies, including BP, took full advantage of their access, offering up suggestions for policy changes—such as tax breaks and lighter environmental regulations—that would help their businesses produce more energy at lower cost. While Cheney refused to release the names of the people and companies that advised the task force, BP acknowledged in 2005 that its executives participated. John Browne, on February 23, 2001, met with Energy Secretary Spencer Abraham on a visit to Washington, according to Energy Department records.

On March 20 of that year, the American Petroleum Institute (API) provided a draft Executive Order to the Energy Department that would require federal agencies such as the Environmental Protection Agency to consider the energy supply impact of any regulations. Two months later, President Bush issued Executive Order 13211 that did just that. Bush's order echoed the API draft almost verbatim in some sections.

A week later, on March 27, the National Petroleum Council, of which BP was a member, gave a presentation to the task force about the increasing demand for natural gas and the resources, including hundreds of thousands of miles of pipeline, access to offshore fields, and a better workforce, necessary to meet it.

Cheney's report, issued in May, warned that blackouts were likely again that summer and that U.S. consumption of oil would rise by

33 percent, from its current 19.5 million barrels a day, and natural gas use would rise 50 percent by 2020. The 105 recommendations included creating economic incentives to promote exploration and development of high-cost oil fields, including deepwater fields, and to review the policies barring offshore exploration in some areas of the outer continental shelf.

The report was met with derision by environmentalists who said it was too focused on boosting supply of fossil fuels at the expense of promoting alternative forms of energy. They also groused that Cheney had refused to meet with them altogether.

The economy, in the meantime, had slid into recession and persistent high energy prices brought up the specter of "stagflation," the economic phenomenon of rising prices accompanying economic stagnation that saps consumer purchasing power, cuts business confidence, and can spur a cycle of economic underperformance. Stagflation in the late 1970s killed the presidency of Jimmy Carter.

"We import 56 percent of our oil, compared with 36 percent in 1973 during the Arab oil embargo," Texas Senator Kay Bailey Hutchison said at the time. "Greatly curtailing our dependence on foreign sources is the only way to ensure a stable domestic energy market. It keeps jobs in America. America's long-term economic and national security may well depend on it." Lawmakers took up different sides of the energy debate, with Republicans mostly advocating more domestic production of oil and gas and Democrats looking for incentives to develop alternative fuels, such as solar or wind energy.

Then on September 11, 2001, Arab militants, 15 of them from Saudi Arabia, hijacked four jumbo jets in the skies over the United States and crashed them into the World Trade Center towers in New York, the Pentagon, and a field in Pennsylvania. The United States invaded Afghanistan, and then Iraq. A new term entered the popular and political lexicon: energy security.

When the World Trade Center collapsed in flames, the oil underneath the Gulf, and the oil locked under the outer continental shelf elsewhere in the United States, was suddenly more important than ever. The public began to realize that the environmental risks of drilling off U.S. shores had to be balanced with the geopolitical risks of being dependent on oil from hostile or volatile nations such as Iran, Russia, and Nigeria. Until the U.S. consumer was willing to give up cars, big houses, or massive refrigerators, oil was a fact of life.

Congress spent the next two years debating new energy legislation. Oil and gas companies spent $287 million, from 2001 to 2005, lobbying lawmakers and the Bush Administration to implement Cheney's plan. They gave another $29 million to candidates in the 2002 and 2004 election cycles.

At the same time oil prices continued to rise and gasoline prices followed. One truism in U.S. politics is that people vote with their wallets. And politicians, above all, want votes. The potent combination of heavy lobbying, political contributions, and an electorate frustrated by ever-climbing prices at the gas pump prevailed on Capitol Hill. In July 2005, the House and Senate agreed to an energy bill that gave $2.6 billion in subsidies for oil exploration and refining. Still, oil prices continued their upward march.

By the summer of 2008 gas prices exceeded $4 a gallon for the first time and congressional offices were receiving thousands of calls from angry voters who wanted action. When President George W. Bush lifted the presidential ban on new drilling on July 14, 2008, crude oil was $145 a barrel. Now the issue was in the hands of Congress, which had renewed its own prohibition on opening new areas to offshore drilling every year since 1993.

The price spike came in the heat of one of the most heavily contested and closely watched presidential elections in U.S. history. Senator Hillary Clinton, wife of former President Bill Clinton, appeared to have a lock on the Democratic nomination, leaving her poised to become the first woman president of the United States. Then an upstart young African-American senator named Barack Obama stole the hearts of young liberals. His messages of hope and change inspired voters more than Clinton's pragmatic message of experience and sense. Obama, born of a black Kenyan father and a white American mother, could also make history as the first African-American president, if he prevailed over Clinton and the Republican nominee.

John McCain, a lionized war hero, was known in Congress for voting his own way despite what party leaders wanted. In 2000 he launched an unorthodox and underfunded campaign against Bush, the choice of the Republican establishment, driving around the country in a bus he dubbed the "Straight Talk Express." He was unsuccessful and returned to the Capitol. In 2008, however, he pulled the old bus out again, and tried for a second trek to the White House. His campaign was left for dead early on, when he ran out of money and fired most of his staff. Then, as opponent after opponent imploded, McCain was the last man standing.

For voters the choice was stark. They could back a conservative white man, a war hero, a known quantity. Or they could vote for one of two known liberals and make history with either choice.

For the oil industry, the stakes were high. Would the United States continue the agenda set by Bush and Cheney, focusing on finding more domestic fossil fuels and protecting the oil supplied abroad through diplomacy or force? Or would the current support for domestic exploration be redirected to alternative energy sources?

When the $4 per gallon prices started showing up on signs at filling stations across the country, and cable television channels showed film of them round the clock, the voters' anger moved toward supporting more domestic energy exploration.

Washington-based interest groups spent millions, and used new tools available via the World Wide Web, to harness the anger. Newt Gingrich, former House speaker, began a "Drill Here, Drill Now, Lower Prices" campaign through his American Solutions groups. The group gathered more than 1 million signatures in favor of offshore drilling.

Actor Chuck Norris, who had been an outspoken supporter of former Arkansas Governor Mike Huckabee's presidential campaign, filmed a video for YouTube showing him filling up the tank of a pickup truck and complaining it cost $82.52, "and I'm only at a quarter of a tank." "I'd like to roundhouse kick this pump to the next county," he says, and goes on to blame Congress. "They've got their heads up their butts. Let's tell Congress we're the bosses, they're not."

Country singer Aaron Tippin recorded an anthem titled "Drill Here, Drill Now." The video included satirical photos of signs at gas stations showing the price for a gallon of regular gasoline was one arm, while it took a leg to get a gallon of plus. Premium would cost your first-born.

Obama appeared to oppose expanding drilling. On June 20, 2008, in a campaign event in Jacksonville, Florida, he had declared "offshore drilling would not lower gas prices today. It would not lower gas prices tomorrow. It would not lower gas prices this year. It would not lower gas prices five years from now."

Still, high gas prices cause a particular sort of anger in American drivers, and American voters, says Larry Sabato, a political scientist at the University of Virginia. "All of us drive to work. You're constantly filling up and you look up at the numbers," he says. "It's a daily irritant. People go to gas stations more than they go to the grocery store."

Opinion polls showed voters, who until that summer had rarely thought about offshore oil, wanting more drilling. About two-thirds of likely voters in a Rasmussen poll said in June 2008 they wanted to see more drilling off the coasts of California, Florida and other states. More than half said drilling would lower gas prices. By July, even California voters were turning. For the first time in 30 years, more than half of those polled by the Public Policy Institute of California said they favored more offshore drilling. And in August, 63 percent of Americans said they backed offshore drilling in areas that were at that time off limits.

There was little talk about safety by either side. It had been almost 20 years since the Exxon Valdez, and nearly 40 since the Santa Barbara spill. So many wells had been drilled in the Gulf waters without large-scale disasters that the companies, the voters, and the politicians had convinced themselves that offshore oil exploration and extraction were safe. "We got to the point where going down into 5,000 feet of water to drill oil wells became no big deal, probably because no one had ever seen a worst-case scenario actually play out before," said Carl Larry, president of Oil Outlooks & Opinions LLC in Houston.

In 2008, the American Petroleum Institute, an industry trade group, launched a series of ads extolling the benefits of domestic oil and natural gas production, from increased jobs to lower prices. The ads also tried to impress and reassure the public with claims about drilling and undersea technology. "One platform can now gather oil from wells 40 miles away," says the narrator, a blond woman in a dark business suit, in an ad entitled High-Tech Subsea Production. "That's more of the oil and natural gas we need, from less than meets the eye." Even opponents of offshore drilling didn't raise the possibility of catastrophe, but rather of incremental damage to the environment and wildlife. The Center for Biological Diversity, for example, seized on the potential of seismic testing hurting sperm whales in its opposition to offshore drilling.

Congress debated through the summer whether to renew the drilling ban. Opponents of more drilling in the outer continental shelf lobbied them individually and hard. Still, they could see the tide turning against them.

To help keep track of where they stood, lobbyists rated lawmakers on a scale of one to five: "one" for drilling opponents and "five" for the strongest advocates for opening up the outer continental shelf to oil companies. For lobbyists, the game typically focuses on winning over the twos and threes.

Democrats tried to fight the tide with studies like one in 2007 from the nonpartisan Energy Information Administration that found more offshore drilling wouldn't do much to boost production or lower prices until about 2030. House Speaker Nancy Pelosi called the link between offshore drilling and lower prices a "hoax." Nothing worked. By mid-summer, the twos and threes were slipping away.

"You'd walk into their offices, and they'd say, 'It's going to be really hard to help you out,'" said Michael Gravitz, Oceans Advocate at the nonprofit advocacy group Environment America.

The economy was in freefall and voters didn't want to see prices rise any more. They wanted to see the government do something to help create jobs. John McCain seized on the combination of an economic recession and rising gas prices to press his advantage on this issue against Obama, who by late summer had locked up the Democratic nomination. In one campaign ad, a narrator intoned: "With gas prices soaring, Barack Obama says no to offshore drilling and says he'll raise taxes on electricity? Higher taxes, more foreign oil, that's the real Obama."

Within the Obama campaign there was a tug-of-war between the energy policy advisers, who wanted to see a thoughtful and nuanced policy, and the pollsters and political advisers who were afraid attacks like McCain's would hurt their candidate. The policy wonks won out in an early battle when Obama refused to go along with a proposal advocated by McCain and Hillary Clinton to declare a gas-tax holiday to offer relief at the pump. With offshore drilling, the wonks and pollsters eventually moved to the same side.

While Obama was originally opposed to expanding exploration on the outer continental shelf, his energy advisers saw it could be part of a plan that would work to move the country away from fossil fuels, while recognizing that they were needed for at least another two decades. In a meeting just before an energy speech at Cape Canaveral, Florida, his team convinced the future president that it was time to open the door to drilling and then use it as a chip to win support for a law that would address global warming. That it might neutralize the campaign issue was an added bonus.

The following day, Obama told reporters in a press conference that, while he remained "skeptical," he'd be willing to support an expansion of "careful and responsible" offshore drilling as part of an energy bill that also dealt with climate change.

Republicans weren't appeased. Republican National Committee Chairman Michael Steele coined the autumn rallying cry when, at the party convention in St. Paul, Minnesota, he told voters it was time to reduce dependence on foreign oil and get the energy that was already in the United States "Let me make it very clear. Drill, baby, drill, and drill now!" he said, as the crowd chanted "Drill, baby, drill!" along with him. The chant was repeated at campaign events for Republican nominee John McCain and his newly chosen running mate, who came from one of the country's biggest oil states, Alaska Governor Sarah Palin.

Palin seized on the slogan and the issue. Alaska, which doesn't charge residents any income, sales or property tax, took in about $11 billion in 2008 in royalties from oil companies, almost double the entire state budget. Each Alaska resident receives an annual check from the state, their individual share of the oil riches. Still, large areas of Alaska, including the Arctic National Wildlife Refuge in the north, had been cordoned off from new oil exploration.

In a rally in Carson, California, just a month before Election Day, Palin worked the crowd into a frenzied chant in support of oil drilling. Prices are going up, and paychecks are shrinking, she told her supporters, all because of high energy costs. The situation was ridiculous, she told, them "when you consider the wealth of natural resources that god has so richly blessed this land with. We have billions of barrels of oil and hundreds of millions of cubic feet of clean green natural gas." The crowd interrupted her with chants of "Drill, baby, drill!" as she beamed from the stage in her green jacket and black skirt. Then she gave them what they wanted.

"We will drill here, and drill now," she said with a smile. "And now's when you start that chant: Drill, baby, drill." The crowd complied and Palin chuckled, "You guys are great!"

Obama, outflanked, quietly put out the word to Democratic leaders on the Hill to put the issue to rest and repeal the drilling ban. By the end of September, the moratorium was gone. Lawmakers allowed it to lapse when they approved the budget for the Department of Interior without the language that had been there for the previous two decades.

● ● ●

Oil prices receded from the political debate during the same month when Wall Street investment bank Lehman Brothers Holdings Inc. went bankrupt, sending the entire U.S. financial system into a tailspin. Voters whose top concern had been the cost of filling their gas tank were now worried whether their banks would stay in business, and whether their jobs were safe.

Obama's cool demeanor inspired greater confidence in voters than McCain's emotional, gut instincts. On November 4, 2008, Obama won the White House. The economy was in freefall and stabilizing the financial system was the top of his agenda. The oil debate hadn't disappeared completely, however.

Just four days before Obama took office, President George W. Bush threw down a gauntlet. He issued a five-year plan that opened vast areas of the Outer Continental Shelf, from Alaska to the Atlantic Coast, to exploration. Obama's new interior secretary, Ken Salazar, immediately delayed the plan and opened it up to public comment for an additional six months.

Salazar and his seven siblings grew up on a ranch with no electricity or telephone in Colorado's San Luis Valley. The former Colorado senator was no knee-jerk liberal who was opposed to oil; he often wears a cowboy hat and traces his roots to the conquistadors who settled the west before it was part of the United States. He was known as a steward of the environment, but he also believed in using the nation's natural resources. In the six months after becoming interior secretary, Salazar hosted meetings around the country, and ordered scientific reviews, to determine how to proceed with offshore oil exploration.

He was skewered by the industry. "Secretary Salazar's announcement means that development of our offshore resources could be stalled indefinitely," the American Petroleum Institute said in a press release in February 2009. "That would delay Americans' access to nearly 160,000 new, well-paying jobs, $1.7 trillion in revenues to federal, state and local governments and greater energy security."

Reviewing the leasing plan wasn't the only thing on Salazar's agenda, however. Responsibility for overseeing oil rights, both on land and offshore, fell to the Minerals Management Service (MMS), an agency within Salazar's department that was at best in disarray and, at worst, utterly corrupt.

An inspector general report in 2008 showed that MMS managers who were tasked with collecting royalties from oil companies had sexual relationships with industry officials, bought drugs—referred to as "office supplies"—from subordinates, and accepted cash and gifts from oil company employees. That report came two years after revelations that the agency mistakenly eliminated a provision in its offshore drilling leases for two years that would have increased royalties for oil recovered in the Gulf of Mexico as prices rose. When the price for a barrel surged from $10 to more than $50, the agency lost as much as $7 billion because of the error. A report in 2010 showed that MMS workers in Lake Charles, Louisiana, some of whom were assigned to inspect offshore drilling platforms in the Gulf of Mexico, accepted gifts from oil and gas companies. A culture of complacency permeated the agency, where officials saw their mandate as promoting the interests of the oil industry and bringing in revenue to the agency in the form of lease payments and royalties. They appeared to treat drilling a mile underwater as routine.

So even as Salazar began work revamping the troubled agency, he didn't slow the offshore exploration that was already underway. On Feb. 23, 2009, 33 days after Obama's inauguration, BP asked the Minerals Management Service for permission to search the nine-square-mile section of the sea floor, known as Mississippi Canyon 252, for crude. The 52-page proposal included an environmental impact analysis that acknowledged the danger to wildlife, beaches, and wetlands. The company repeatedly noted, however, that due to the 48-mile distance from the shoreline and its response capabilities in the event of a spill, "no significant adverse impacts are expected."

MMS approved the plan to drill two wells beneath 4,992 feet of water six weeks later in a six-sentence letter that urged the company to "exercise caution" because of "indications of shallow gas and possible water flow." Agency officials had become so comfortable with offshore drilling that they failed to perform even the most perfunctory check to ensure that the drilling rig's safety equipment was functional. Frank Patton, the MMS drilling engineer who granted BP the permit to drill the Macondo well, never asked the company to include proof that the two-foot-long blades—known as shear rams—that cut a pipe and crimp a well shut in case of an emergency would work.

Shear rams are part of the blowout preventer, a safety device that's the last line of defense against a catastrophic blowout. The problem is, blowout preventers often fail, and the shear rams don't work properly at least half the time. The MMS knew this—it was their own study that revealed it. Instead of requiring the industry to come up with better safety devices, the agency, in 2002, began requiring companies to certify that their shear rams would actually cut the pipe when triggered. Patton, however, who was in charge of most of the Gulf operations for MMS, didn't know about the requirement. "I was never told to look for this statement," Patton told Coast Guard investigators at a hearing a month after the Deepwater Horizon exploded. Documents show MMS also exempted the oil company from conducting an environmental impact review, a requirement of the National Environmental Protection Act. David Pettit, an attorney at the Natural Resources Defense Council, said such exemptions were standard practice.

"This was a bunch of people who were very sympathetic to the industry and shared its values," said Petitt.

BP did have a detailed strategy to clean up any oil that hit the water in case of a blowout. In the 582-page plan filed with MMS, BP said it could handle a blowout that would spew 250,000 barrels of crude oil into the Gulf of Mexico a day. Given what happened after the Macondo blowout, BP's plan, which was almost identical to one filed by every major oil company operating in the Gulf, was full of fantastic claims.

The company claimed, among other things, that skimming vessels stationed around the Gulf could suck up 491,721 barrels of oil a day. Yet six weeks after the Macondo well blew out, skimmers, specialized boats that sweep oil off the surface of the water, had picked up a total of 312,952 barrels of oily water mixture. "That's not all oil, it's oily water," BP spokesman John Curry explained at the time.

The company also said there was little danger to the shorelines because of the distance of the well. There was a 20 percent chance that the oil would reach Plaquemines Parish a month after a Macondo blowout, BP's response plan said. Plaquemines residents found oil in their marshes in mid-May. Eventually crude oil and tar balls reached the shorelines in five states, killed countless birds and fish, and shut down much of the Gulf's fishing grounds for months. Four months after the blowout, scientists claimed that a plume of oil the size of Manhattan remained deep below the surface. The response plan was "a bald-faced, flat out lie," said Carl Pope, chairman of the Sierra Club.

Hayward acknowledged the company wasn't prepared to clean up a catastrophic oil spill. "What is undoubtedly true is that we did not have the tools you would want in your tool-kit," he said in June.

MMS also knew that the cleanup claims were fiction. BP's emergency plan involved skimmers, booms, and dispersants. The first two were only effective against oil on the surface of the water. They did nothing to contain the spread of oil that spewed from the mile-deep well and remained below. The capabilities of skimmers were also a matter of ongoing debate in the industry. The vessels were originally rated as if they were likely to suck pure oil out of the water, rather than the crude mixed with water that would actually be vacuumed up. Some companies adjusted their skimmer ratings to take the water into account, but even the adjusted ratings don't reflect reality, some critics say.

Eric Heinitz, an environmental specialist for the State of Washington who has consulted on oil spill cleanup for 25 years, says current ratings don't take into account the time it takes for the vessel to travel from the shore to the oil, and to move from oil slick to oil slick. "You can put the skimmer in the water, but if there's not oil there, you're not going to skim oil."

Still, MMS approved the plan, which covered not only the Macondo exploration well but every well BP was drilling in the Gulf. The plan listed walruses, seals, and sea lions among the wildlife in the Gulf, suggesting they copied much of the scenario from their Arctic plans. Most of the major oil companies, including Exxon, had submitted identical response plans, all of them mentioning walruses and seals.

● ● ●

Long before Salazar had made any fundamental changes at the MMS, Obama decided to take action on offshore drilling.

On March 31, 2010, the president strode to a podium in a hangar at Andrews Air Force Base in Maryland, and announced that he'd open new areas to drilling off the mid- and south-Atlantic coast and the Gulf of Mexico as part of a broader energy security plan.

"Today we're announcing the expansion of offshore oil and gas exploration, but in ways that balance the need to harness domestic energy resources and the need to protect America's natural resources," said the president, who stood before an F-18 fighter jet called the Green Hornet that can fly using biofuels. As Obama spoke, workers on the Deepwater Horizon were already losing control of the Macondo well.

It was Congressional politics that drove the decision to make the speech. The president wanted to rewrite the energy policies passed in the Bush years to reflect his own belief that the United States needed to deal with the threat of climate change—he wanted to put a price on carbon. To bring enough members of Congress on board, he would have to allow drilling off the coast of the Southeastern United States, where some geologists think there could be substantial oil deposits. Then he could win some Southern Republicans to his side.

By Spring 2009 the financial crisis and recession had driven gas prices down from their highs of the campaign summer. Still, drilling remained central to discussions in Washington as Democrats tried to gather support for an energy bill that would address climate change by putting a price on carbon emissions and promoting alternatives to petroleum.

Oil industry officials argued persuasively that short supplies and rising energy prices could short-circuit an economic recovery. "The facts are nonpartisan," said Larry Nichols, CEO of Houston-based Devon Energy Corp., the biggest independent oil company. "We need all the sources of energy we can get in this country, including oil and natural gas."

They also spent heavily lobbying politicians. Oil and gas companies spent $134,475,402 in the election year of 2008, and then ramped up their efforts, spending $175,079,824 in 2009 as Congress began to debate energy and climate legislation. BP's lobbying mirrored industry patterns, with the company laying out $10.5 million in 2008 and boosting that to $16 million in 2009. It was the fourth biggest spender in the industry, exceeded by ExxonMobil, Chevron, and ConocoPhillips.

In April 2008, Senator John Kerry, a Massachusetts Democrat, stopped his Republican colleague from South Carolina, Lindsey Graham, on the Senate floor and asked if they could meet to discuss an energy bill. The two got together a few days later and agreed to work out a bill that would place a price on carbon emissions, and allow new offshore oil exploration. Both men were "going into their zones of discomfort," Kerry told his staff. Graham would only play ball if offshore drilling was included in the deal. With the moratorium lifted, Graham wanted to create a system where states that wanted drilling off their coasts could share in the riches that came out of the ground. For years, Alaska had luxuriated in the steady cash flow of its oil royalties and South Carolinians should have the same privilege, Graham reasoned.

"Lindsey Graham really guided this debate in terms of new drilling," said Athan Manuel, Director of the Lands Protection Program at the Sierra Club in Washington. "He's the guy who put it on the table and kept it on the table. John Kerry, who voted against offshore drilling for 30 years, was willing to hold his nose and go along."

Graham immediately became crucial to Obama's agenda because he was the only Republican willing to talk. The administration, said Graham, was happy to oblige. "The president has been great to work with on energy and climate. I want to say this about the administration, they've been very reasonable on offshore drilling," he told reporters outside the White House on March 10, 2010.

That same day, the Deepwater Horizon reported to the Minerals Management Service that its well was in trouble. "We are in the midst of a well control situation on MC 252 #001 and have stuck pipe," BP's Scherie Douglas said in an e-mail to Frank Patton, using the shorthand for Mississippi Canyon 252. "We are bringing out equipment to begin operations to sever the drill pipe, plug back the well, and bypass."

●●●

Members of Congress and the White House weren't aware of the volatile situation in the Gulf. They were aware, however, of their perilous position in the upcoming congressional elections, where analysts were predicting major losses for Democrats, who at the time controlled both the House and Senate. Environmentalists said Democrats accepted off-shore drilling as the price for getting a climate bill passed, and because they feared a return of the "Drill, baby, drill!" chants of two years earlier. So the White House decided to go on the offensive, having Obama announce his own drilling plan that would put him squarely on the side of offshore drilling, while allowing states like California and Massachusetts, who were opposed to oil rigs off their beaches, to opt out.

Twenty days later, the Deepwater Horizon exploded in a ball of flames over the ocean, sending Michael Williams, Stephen Bertone and more than a hundred others fleeing into the sea. Obama could no longer point the finger at George W. Bush. Offshore drilling was now his baby.

Within days of the explosion an e-mail was circulating on the Internet with a photo of the Deepwater Horizon in flames in the middle of the ocean, surrounded by firefighting ships spraying water on the rig. The caption read: "Drill, baby, drill!"

Chapter 6

Lord Browne's Long Goodbye

After the Russia deal, John Browne probably should have focused on smoothing out all the rough edges resulting from the many take-overs. In a sense that was the goal he set himself. A confidential presentation to the board in September 2003 spelled out BP's strategy. The company had grown rapidly through deals, it said, "We now need to make what we have work." That isn't what happened.

Instead, in the ensuing years, BP threatened to come apart at the seams as its race to grow produced a series of accidents and other mis-haps. Browne seemed to run out of gas. His takeover strategies were no longer a surprise, and they weren't as suited to an era of higher-priced oil. Yet, according to insiders and the Oil Lord himself, Browne devoted much of his energy in his twilight years to what turned out to be a fruitless effort to merge with Shell in one last glorious deal.

● ● ●

In late July 2006, John Browne and Peter Sutherland, BP's Chairman, held a meeting in the latter's office described in the press as "tense and hostile." Sutherland, who had an easy ride as Chairman during most of Browne's tenure, had grown impatient with his CEO and thought it was time for him to set a retirement date. BP's normal retirement age is 60, which Browne would reach in February 2008.

The boardroom tensions were played out in the press through a series of leaks during the summer of 2006. Both sides anonymously briefed reporters about their positions and BP investors, employees, and other stakeholders were left puzzled about what was transpiring at the top of the company. For instance, a July 24 article in the *Financial Times*, Britain's business daily, told readers that Browne "was expected to announce" that he would retire in February 2008. However, Browne was said to be "keen to leave open the possibility that investor pressure will eventually pressure the board to extend his tenure."

Just who was behind these stories was hard to pin point. Associates of Browne had been campaigning for him to stay on in the top job. Some financial groups rallied to the cause. Merrill Lynch, for instance, put out a research note calling the succession issue "a potential medium term risk for shareholders." Browne, himself, had given a speech complaining of age discrimination at the restored Wilton's Music Hall in the East End of London. "A truly civilized society is one in which people have genuine choices unfettered by their color, their origins, or their age," he said, attracting plenty of press attention.

Sutherland, a burly former rugby player, who had parlayed his political savvy as an E.U. Commissioner into the chairs of Goldman Sachs International and BP, was having none of it. Pressing Browne to make a clear statement about his intentions, Sutherland, a former Irish attorney general, warned Browne that otherwise he might go nuclear. It was a humiliating moment for the proud BP CEO, but worse was to come.

If Browne thought there was a realistic possibility of extending his term he was overestimating the support he enjoyed on BP's board.

He may have transformed the company. But unlike a few years earlier, when he could do no wrong, BP had been hit by a series of disasters and scandals that had tarnished his image. In his book Browne admits to self-delusion and says that it was time to go. "However, my emotional self prevailed over reason," he says.

● ● ●

Much had changed since Browne's triumphant foray in Russia three years before. What happened on March 23, 2005, at a BP refinery not far from Houston was responsible for much of that shift. On that day a geyser of high-octane fuel shot 20 feet high from a 113-foot-tall stack at BP's refinery in Texas City, Texas, and spewed combustible liquid and vapors across a 200,000 square foot area. The vapors found a spark that ignited the fuel. A series of explosions leveled and charred a large section of the 1,200-acre refinery, vaporized a portable office trailer on the site, and shattered windows in houses that were nearly a mile away. Fifteen people were killed and more than 180 were injured, many seriously.

Dave Senko was the project manager with Jacobs Engineering, a contractor that worked regularly at the Texas City refinery. On March 23, 2005, he had about 700 workers at the site, including about 400 in the ultracracker unit converting an older steam compressor to an electric version. That unit was adjacent to the isomerization plant, which makes high-octane fuel to blend with gasoline, where the accident happened.

Senko was in Los Angeles that morning visiting BP's Carson refinery, where workers were complaining that conditions were unsafe and an accident could happen at any moment. "It was the worst construction workplace that I had ever seen anywhere in the world," Senko said in an interview. He said people at Carson were working in deep trenches that had not been shored up to meet California's earthquake standards. The smell of hydrocarbons was so strong that it made him nauseous, and there was open electrical work that could have set off the fuel vapors at any time, he said. He shut down work, got in a van, and headed to the BP management office to discuss the problems. "It was unacceptable on BP's side; it was unacceptable on the Jacobs side. I was going to fire a bunch of people," he said.

Instead, his phone rang. It was his wife calling. There had been a massive explosion at Texas City. She saw it on the news. She had forgotten he was out of town. She just wanted to hear his voice. Senko blew off the meeting with BP's Carson management and headed for Los Angeles International Airport. Then his boss called and told him again about the blast. It was bad, he said. There would be fatalities. "Dave, I need to know who was in the trailer," he said. Jacobs had a mobile trailer with a dozen offices for construction managers sitting just outside the isomerization unit. Senko had no idea who was there that morning. Several people had offices in the trailer, and many others were in there routinely. Anyone could be there anytime on odd business.

"I hung up with him and I decide I'm going to call my three top guys who always answer their cell phones. I called Morris King, my project manager. No answer. Then I dial Larry Thomas, the project super. No answer. Then I try Eugene White, the safety coordinator. No answer," Senko recalls. "When I didn't reach those three that's what told me it was serious." He would later learn that all three men were dead.

Senko landed in Houston at 11 P.M., nine hours after the explosion. His boss told him investigators were keeping them from the refinery grounds so he should go home, rest, and come back at 4 A.M. "Tomorrow is going to be a day you're never going to forget," his supervisor said, and signed off. Senko spent the next several hours in his living room watching videos of news coverage of the explosion that his wife had taped on their VCR. What he learned: The trailer where Jacobs' construction managers had their offices had been destroyed.

When Senko got to the refinery in the pre-dawn hours, he went to relieve a colleague who had spent the night at the helipad identifying injured workers as he helped load them onto life flight helicopters.

The choppers were shuttling back and forth from local hospitals all night. "We still at that point had a lot of people missing and unidentified. It was a mess," said Senko.

As Senko spent the morning looking at maimed and burned men and women, John Browne arrived to tour the site and meet with officials and refinery workers. At a press conference at the city hall later that afternoon Browne said, "Yesterday was a dark day in BP's history. It is the worst tragedy I have known in my time with the company." Sitting in the mayor's chair in the city council chambers in a neat grey suit, Browne said the company had done all it could to ensure the refinery was safe. "There was no limit to the amount of activity that we've undertaken in Texas City to make it a very safe plant, and it is a very safe plant." He vowed that BP would find out what happened. "We are responsible for what happens inside the boundaries of our plant, and this is no exception," he said.

Brown said the company couldn't mend what had happened the day before, but promised to help the victims and their families. "What we can do is to bring our resources to bear to help in however way we can do it, to make their future feel a bit better, make their tomorrow a bit better than yesterday," he said. "BP in its way, using the resources of the company, fully intends to do that. That's what we do."

Senko meantime went to the convention center in Texas City where a room was set up to help the families of the 15 people who remained missing. Eleven of them were Jacobs employees who worked for Senko. He said he couldn't tell the families any information until the coroner had formally identified the bodies. "Families were calling about the status, we couldn't tell them anything," Senko said. "Even what we did know we couldn't tell them. I knew Ryan Rodriguez had died, but I couldn't say anything." Officials had accounted for all but 15 people at the plant that day. However, they had only recovered 14 bodies. That discrepancy gave each of the families gathered at round tables at the convention center a ray of hope that their missing relative might be found alive in the wreckage, or unaccounted for in a nearby hospital. "They were all thinking, hoping, praying that their person missing would show up somewhere," Senko said.

One by one, the families were called and taken by van to the nearby Mainland Medical Center to identify their loved ones. "When we announced that we had found the 15th body, it was terrible. Everyone knew that their missing person was also dead."

Before the day ended, Houston attorney Terry Bryant was in court filing the first of hundreds of lawsuits on behalf of workers injured in the blast.

● ● ●

There were plenty of people angry at BP over the Texas City disaster. Browne's particular nemesis was a flamboyant personal injury lawyer named Brent Coon from Beaumont, Texas. Coon's telephone began ringing within days of the massive blast. When Coon took on his first Texas City refinery clients, he had no idea the case would consume years of his life. Soon after the disaster, when it became clear there would be hundreds of claims against the company, Coon was designated lead counsel of the Plaintiff's Steering Committee. He became the face of the Texas City victims.

Relaxed in the penthouse living quarters that he keeps above his Houston office, Coon's blond hair falls straight across his forehead. When he's on television, as he is frequently, that hair is brushed back with a slight wave, apparently aided by styling cream. On a hot August Friday afternoon, he was wearing black boots, jeans with brightly-colored stitching on the back pockets, and a sleeveless T-shirt that revealed a large tattoo on one shoulder. The shirt read: "If you give a Big Dog a steak, he'll eat for a day. If you teach a Big Dog to barbecue, he'll sit by the grill and drink beer all weekend."

Coon's Houston bachelor pad is sumptuously decorated in a kind of nouveau Henry VIII style with lots of dark carved wood, tapestries, massive leather couches, and marble statuary. On his desk is an auto-graphed photo of a nude model. There's a crystal decanter etched with the Houston Texans football team logo, flat screens mounted on walls between heavy velvet drapes and a room with only a round card table. Wine bottles laid on their sides fill a large glass-fronted cabinet. The refrigerator is well stocked with beer.

When it comes to BP, however, he's all business. His knowledge of the Texas City case and company is encyclopedic. His key tactic: Blame the mayhem that occurred that day on John Browne. "Lord Browne was responsible. I should not even honor him by calling him by that title," Coon says. "His fingerprints were all over Texas City." Though Coon never met Browne, he became obsessed with the powerful CEO, and did all he could to embarrass him and the company, including releas-ing thousands of internal BP documents that made the man and the company look ruthless. Coon has plenty of incentive to paint BP in its worst light. Plaintiff's lawyers collected close to $2 billion from BP for their clients, and he has clearly done very well for himself out of Texas City, with a historic building in downtown Houston and a luxurious if somewhat offbeat lifestyle that includes a box at Houston Texans football games, motorcycle riding, and playing in a rock band. Most people find downtown Houston boring, especially on weekends, but Coon says he and his friends find all sorts of ways to get in trouble.

Still, many of his assertions are echoed by the several official investigations into the blast. The U.S. Chemical Safety Board, a U.S. government agency which investigates industrial accidents, and a com-mission led by former Secretary of State James Baker, both concluded that BP under Browne was focused too much on boosting produc-tion, cutting costs and increasing profits, and not enough on safety. BP's own internal report said the company directed too little money to maintenance and repairs and that the safety culture at the refinery was troubled.

Those reports were damaging to BP's image, certainly. Coon's were more so, however. He released documents day by day to ensure the disaster remained in the news. And his releases were far more colorful than the bureaucrat-speak that permeated the official findings of the investigators. For example, one document Coon released shows a cost benefit analysis of how much to spend on shelters at the refinery illustrated by the three little pigs fairy tale.

Within weeks of the blast, Coon had signed up about 200 clients, including a young woman named Eva Rowe, a wild-child who grew up in a trailer in the tiny town of Hornbeck, Louisiana. Both of Eva's parents were killed in the Jacobs trailer, and the young woman soon became the poster-child of Texas City victims. *Texas Monthly* magazine ran a long story about Rowe called "Eva vs. Goliath." Coon, who was just one of dozens of attorneys in Houston suing BP, had a staff of 25 people working full-time for four years investigating the immediate causes of the explosion and looking at the behavior of BP's executives in the years since it acquired Amoco Co. and the refinery. To Coon the case became personal. He worked long days, seven days a week. "It was the only case the firm could handle. Usually we have several going at a time but we couldn't do anything else for years," he said. "BP had so much at stake; billions of dollars, their reputation."

It was a year after the explosion before Coon began to see what he believed to be the root cause of the problems at Texas City. He reached back in time and found the people who managed the refinery in 1998 when BP bought Amoco and with it the massive Texas City facility.

Texas City is BP's largest U.S. refinery and the third largest in the country. It can process 475,000 barrels of crude a day, and is capable of supplying 3 percent of the country's gasoline. There were about 2,300 BP employees and more than 3,000 outside contractors working there on a daily basis.

Coon began deposing former employees, most of whom were fired long before. Then he asked for documents, financial records, memos and e-mails. In total, the discovery produced about seven million documents going back years. Coon says BP cut its refining budget to the bone, and disregarded worker safety in the process. "That was insane. That wasn't just a bad idea, that was idiotic," says Coon. "You can't just cut 25 percent out of the costs of your refinery. All your assets will fall apart. All your shit will rust out and it will blow up!"

Coon and his clients argued that the cause of the accident was more than just an error by the refinery operator but went to the heart of the culture of BP. To press his point, he continued to demand documents, hold press conferences and parade the orphaned Eva Rowe before TV cameras. The young woman wanted to hold BP's feet to the fire, and Coon advised her that she could seek a settlement that would make public what they thought was a mass of accumulated evidence about the unsafe practices of the petrochemical industry.

who Coon became fixated on John Browne, whom he saw as an elitist that didn't understand the dangers posed by some of the installations under his management. "Lord Browne had a fundamental disrespect and lack of appreciation for the volatility and dangers of petrochemicals," Coon said. He wanted to question the CEO, but BP fought the request. Coon initially agreed to forego a Browne deposition when the company claimed that he wasn't involved in the day-to-day operations of the refinery. Browne, however, began making the rounds on television, defending BP's conduct in Texas. Coon went to court and eventually won the right from the Texas Supreme Court to question Browne for one hour by telephone. During the deposition, Coon had a courier deliver autopsy photos of Eva Rowe's parents to Browne and went on to question him about the photos. In his testimony, Browne said he ordered the cost cuts in the refining unit after the merger with Amoco because the company didn't compare favorably with competitors in the industry. He said he was not aware of how the Texas City refinery implemented the targets and what specific programs, jobs, and maintenance were cut. However, regulators and internal BP documents do show that Browne's cost cutting took a toll on BP's operations. Texas City came to BP in its 1998 deal with Amoco. The following year, Browne ordered company officials to slash costs by 25 percent across BP's refineries unit. Added to the 41 percent cuts done over the previous years at Amoco, the refineries were under great strain. A 1999 business plan said the South Houston facility had cut costs by $60 million in a year and that Browne had laid out a goal to cut them another 25 percent by 2001.

Internal memos showed the pressure managers were under. A March 1999 memo from the Texas City business unit's vice president, Tim Scruggs, laid out a proposal to cut cash expenses by 10 percent, or $52.6 million, in one year with measures that included deferring $8.3 million in refinery maintenance and reducing the salaried work-force by 10 percent. "Having achieved significant refinery head-count reduction over the past five years, we would have a major challenge for getting the required work completed with the full 10 percent less refinery salaried employees," Scruggs wrote.

In November 2000, the unit was asked to cut another $8 million from its costs before the end of the year. Mark Politte, an operations manager, pushed back against the cuts in a memo that included an analysis of the refinery's budget. "If we accept that operations costs are 'fixed' costs that we cannot readily change, then most of the decrease of $8MM must come from routine maintenance."

Texas City wasn't alone. An internal memo to the company's Grangemouth, Scotland, refinery leaders said Browne had announced a plan to cut $4 billion off the company's costs worldwide, including $1.4 billion from refining and marketing. That refinery had also had safety problems, and a BP internal report concluded that safety "was unofficially sacrificed to cost reductions, and cost pressures inhibited staff from asking the right questions."

In 2002, three years after BP bought Amoco, the cost cuts started anew. Donald Parus, Texas City's manager, warned the South Houston leadership team in an October memo that the unit's results were more than $100 million below the company's forecast of $214.3 million. "Faced with these challenges, we've been asked to take some tempo-rary but drastic steps to stop the bleeding."

● ● ●

Employees may have bristled at the cuts, but analysts loved Browne's work and Wall Street rewarded him by bidding up the stock price. BP's London shares had hovered around 450 pence through 1998 and soared to 638 pence in 1999. The share price averaged about 575 for the next three years.

Browne, who came up through BP's ranks on the exploration and production side, clearly relished that part of the business which took him to exotic parts of the world where he could work his charm on politicians, dictators, and kings. And as Inglis laid out in his "BP 101" lecture, Browne believed that the key to BP's success in the future was finding and exploiting huge new oil fields. To the romantic adventurer, the nuts and bolts of refining may have been less interesting. Oil prices, which bottomed at around $10 in December 1998, began a long march upward, reaching $37 by 2000, and $77 by July 2006. The rise gave BP's upstream businesses, such as exploration and development, huge returns and it helped make the Amoco and Arco deals, concluded at much lower prices, look very smart. Meanwhile the refining and marketing side known as downstream, which in recent years had been a weakness for BP, was always something of a stepchild. For 2003, for instance, the company reported $13.9 billion in replacement cost operating profits, an industry metric, for exploration and production compared to $2.3 billion for refining and marketing.

The job of an oil refinery is to take thick heavy crude oil, or the more valuable light sweet variety, and turn it into a product someone can burn for fuel, use as a lubricant, or some other purpose. Depending on the configuration of the refinery, that product can be gasoline, in a variety of grades, diesel, propane, or any number of chemicals derived from petroleum. The massive web of pipes, gauges, valves and flames are designed to be a pressure cooker, cooking the oil, squeezing it, and ultimately "cracking" it into its component parts, which are then mixed together, and mixed with other chemicals, to make specific products. Texas City is one of the most complex refineries in the world, capable of making a variety of fuels and chemical products, depending on the market's needs. The facility takes in three percent of the total U.S. crude production.

Refining is simple in concept. The challenge is keeping all those volatile hydrocarbons under control while exposing them to extreme heat and pressure. To do that the various vessels being heated and pressurized need to be in good working order. The people monitoring the whole apparatus through gauges and remote cameras need to stay alert. At Texas City on the day of the 2005 explosion, some of the monitoring devices were not working, and workers were overtired from working too much, according to an investigation by the U.S. Chemical Safety Board.

● ● ●

Safety problems were not new at Texas City. The year before the explosion, three workers were killed in two separate incidents. In the three prior decades, 23 people died on the job there, or one every 16 months on average. The company was placed on a Labor Department watch list of companies that were deemed "indifferent" to worker safety. BP was the only oil company on the list, John Miles, the federal Occupational Safety and Health Administration regional director, told the Houston Chronicle at the time.

On March 23, 2005, a unit of the refinery called the isomerization unit was restarting after a 30-day outage for maintenance. Such operations are the most dangerous time at refineries. The restart began on the overnight shift and when the day shift took over, a worker charged with filling a tank didn't realize it had already been filled. High-octane fuel overflowed the tank, into a safety tank called a "blowdown drum." That drum was overwhelmed by the amount of overflow and the highly combustible hydrocarbons shot out of a 13-story stack, falling onto the ground and vaporizing, creating a volatile cloud that spread across the area. When the fumes reached an idling pickup truck, they ignited.

An investigation by the Chemical Safety Board was highly critical of BP. "Cost-cutting, failure to invest, and production pressures from BP Group executive managers impaired process safety performance at Texas City," the Board concluded. "Personnel were not encouraged to report safety problems and some feared retaliation for doing so."

The report said that BP considered several measures to make the refinery safer—including replacing the blowdown drum that was the source of the blast with a safer flare system—but repeatedly chose cheaper options.

Employees, including managers, ignored the company's stated safety policies, the board found. During a startup, which is a particularly hazardous time in a refinery, all nonessential workers are supposed to be evacuated. Senko says that he didn't even know the isomerization unit had been shut down, never mind that it was being restarted that day. If he had known, he says, nobody would have been in that trailer. "I wouldn't have had my people there whether BP wanted us there or not. We know better," Senko says.

That was just one oversight. The trailer where Senko's people worked shouldn't have been sited so close to the refinery where an explosion hazard was high. But BP workers never conducted the risk assessment required before putting the trailer in place. The company also went ahead with the startup even though it knew a gauge that measured the amount of liquid in the tank that overflowed was not functioning.

The Chemical Safety Board said BP, over the years, focused too much on personal safety, such as falls, rather than on the safety of the entire system. Their report, released March 20, 2007, detailed repeated internal studies that identified an urgent need for maintenance and repairs at the plant. Those reports were met with promises, followed by budget cuts. The report cited a 2003 presentation by the refinery managers that asked how the plant got into "our intolerable risk situation with the infrastructure assets." The answer, they said, was culture and money.

BP commissioned a separate panel, lead by former Secretary of State James Baker, to look into the company's overall safety culture. That report also found failures. "BP has not provided effective process safety leadership and has not adequately established process safety as a core value across all its five U.S. refineries," it concluded.

● ● ●

Nancy Leveson, an MIT professor, who was a member of the panel, traces some of BP's problems with safety to the pressure the management style installed by Browne put on people fairly far down the corporate ladder.

> BP under Brown had a theory about pushing responsibility "down" in the hierarchy. I kept arguing with them about that during the Baker Panel. At that time, I could not find the word "safety" in the job responsibility for anyone at the corporate level. After Texas City, they created a staff department, but I'm not sure how much impact there was on line operations. They talked a lot about safety ("safety moments" all the time), but I have a feeling that it did not permeate the culture. But I had less contact with them after the Texas City report.
>
> In general, management focuses on the responsibilities you assign to them and on what you are going to hold them accountable for. If you measure occupational (personal) safety and that is the measurement that you reward people by and that they use as their standard of improvement, that is what they will focus on. I personally (during the Baker Panel) thought that was one of the major causes of Texas City.

The company's own internal report detailed the failures of individual managers and executives, recommending that several be fired. The report concluded that at Texas City, "a culture that evolved over the years seemed to ignore risk, tolerated noncompliance, and accepted incompetence—all of which were present on the night shift of March 22 and the day shift of March 23."

In 2006 BP's board cut Browne's bonus in half, to 900,000 pounds (or $1.76 million, at the time), because of the safety problems, and Sutherland said the year's results "can best be described as mixed."

While the various reports' findings were damaging to the company, it was Coon that kept the story alive for years, with a drip, drip, drip release of embarrassing and damaging documents. He made public an e-mail from John Manzoni, head of BP's refining and marketing, showing he had complained that being forced to return to Texas City after the explosion was ruining his family vacation. He released a 2002 BP safety presentation that became known as the "Three Little Pigs" document in which the company compared its decision on what types of temporary trailers to purchase to the decision by the fairy tale characters on whether to use straw, sticks, or bricks to build their homes.

The presentation, quoted next, illustrated the cost-benefit analysis of comparing the expected frequency of a risky event and the degree of risk that event posed.

> **Frequency:** The big bad wolf blows once per piggy lifetime.
> **Consequence:** If the wolf blows down the house, the piggy is gobbled.
> **Maximum Justifiable Spend (MJS):** The piggy considers it's worth $1,000 to save its bacon.
> $$1.0/\text{piggy lifetime} \times \$1,000/\text{piggy life} = \$1,000$$
> Which type of house should piggy build?

It was tasteless and a public relations disaster that BP compared the safety of its workers to fairy tale characters. On top of that the company used an absurdly low figure for the value of a human life presumably to simplify the example. And in the end BP managers didn't even abide by the recommendations the presentation made.

The optimal office trailer at a refinery, in terms of cost and safety, should be made of bricks that can withstand a blast, the document said. Still, three years later, the trailer where 11 workers were killed was a temporary structure made from much weaker materials.

• • •

By the time Browne and Sutherland had their showdown, Texas City wasn't Browne's only problem. In Alaska, the company had been hit by two highly publicized oil spills because of corrosion problems at its Prudhoe Bay oil field, the largest in the country. BP was forced to partly close the field in August 2006, leading to temporary price increases. According to the *Wall Street Journal* outside attorneys traced part of the corrosion problems to BP not properly integrating ARCO after the 1999 merger.

At roughly the same time, regulators alleged that Houston-based energy traders had tried to manipulate the propane market. Browne had built trading in oil and products into a big moneymaker for BP, but it was an activity that worried regulators and led to tangles with them, in part, because BP might be able to alter the supply and demand balance by its own actions. BP admitted it tried to manipulate the propane market in 2003 and 2004 and settled the case with the Justice Department through a deferred prosecution agreement. Browne and Sutherland had reportedly gotten along well in the early days after Sutherland became Chairman of BP in 1997, succeeding David Simon, a longtime colleague of Browne's. But friction between the two strong-willed men increased and not just over the succession. Stung by Texas City and various other mishaps, Browne wanted to do a deal with Shell, repeating the highly successful earlier gambits in his career. When Shell's CEO Phil Watts was forced out over misreporting the size of the company's oil and gas reserves, a window for a merger seemed to open. In his book Browne says that

The Deepwater Horizon oil rig burning in the Gulf of Mexico. On April 20, 2010, the Horizon was drilling the Macondo exploration well for BP when it suffered a blowout and explosion and finally sank.
Source: U.S. Coast Guard.

Workers clean up oil spilled from a corroded BP pipeline that pumps oil from the Prudhoe Bay oil field in Alaska on August 11, 2006.
Source: Kimberly White, Bloomberg News.

D'Arcy's drillers make their first commercial oil discovery in May 1908, at Masjid–i–Sulieman in Southwest Persia.
Source: BP.

William Knox D'Arcy, founder of the Anglo-Persian Oil Company (BP's predecessor).
Source: BP.

John Browne of BP in 2003.
Source: Graham Barclay, Bloomberg News.

Andy Inglis, BP's head of exploration and production when the Deepwater Horizon exploded. His job was eliminated six months later.
Source: BP.

Jeff Chevalier, John Browne's former boyfriend, whom he met through a gay escort service. The image appeared on the Facebook social networking site and was photographed from a computer screen in Berlin, Germany, in 2007.
Source: Adam Berry, Bloomberg News.

Attorney Brent Coon with client Eva Rowe outside the Federal Courthouse in Houston on February 4, 2008.
Source: F. Carter Smith, Bloomberg News.

BP's Thunder Horse platform in the Gulf of Mexico.
Source: BP.

Alaska delegates to the Republican National Convention don T-shirts that say, "Drill baby drill!" on September 4, 2008.
Source: Joshua Roberts, Bloomberg News.

BP CEO Tony Hayward stands in front of a photo of an oil platform at a press conference to announce 2009 profits.
Source: Simon Dawson, Bloomberg News.

Protesters demonstrate outside BP's offices in Washington, D.C., on June 4, 2010.
Source: Andrew Harrer, Bloomberg News.

President Barack Obama, Coast Guard Admiral Thad Allen, and LaFourche Parish President Charlotte Randolph tour an oil-marred beach in Port Fourchon, Louisiana. Obama called the oil spill "an assault on our shores."
Source: Win McNamee, pool photo via Bloomberg.

Tony Hayward and Robert Dudley leave the White House on June 16, 2010, after meeting with President Barack Obama and agreeing to put $20 billion into an oil spill compensation fund.
Source: Andrew Harrer, Bloomberg News.

Robert Dudley (right) speaks to reporters outside BP headquarters after he is named CEO on July 27, 2010. He replaces Tony Hayward (left), who was criticized for mishandling the company's response to the Gulf of Mexico oil spill. At center is BP Chairman Carl-Henric Svanberg.
Source: Rupert Hartley, Bloomberg News.

A mural protesting BP and questioning President Barack Obama is painted outside the Southern Sting Tattoo Parlor in Larose, Louisiana (June 6, 2010).
Source: Derick E. Hingle, Bloomberg News.

not long after becoming BP's CEO in 1995, he received an unwelcome approach from Shell.

Nearly 10 years into his tenure he thought BP was now on a more equal footing with Shell. He broached the idea of a merger with Watts' successor, Jeroen van der Veer, as the two walked in the morning sun along the shores of Lake Como in Italy in June 2004. Browne's plan: Shed all of BP's troubled refining and marketing operations. BP estimated that such a combination would have brought $9 billion in so-called synergies, Browne says. His executive team was on board, he says, but "certain individual BP board members" were not. Browne tried to persuade the board to consider his proposal again at a meeting at Williamsburg, Virginia in September 2005, but the board declined. Another executive says that Sutherland took his own soundings at Shell and found that the company wasn't serious about a merger. Sutherland, who had presided over the creation of much of the European Union's antitrust legislation as Competition Czar, also thought that a Shell/BP combination would struggle to be approved.

While they respected Browne's achievements and business acumen, top Shell executives apparently never took his marriage proposals seriously. They thought accepting his offer in 2004 would be unfair because it would be taking advantage of what would prove a temporary dip in the company's stock price due to the reserve mess. They also doubted that regulators would approve, and they found the cost-savings he proposed extreme. Most important of all, they sensed, partly based on signals from the board, Browne was speaking for himself and not for the whole company.

Relations between Browne and Sutherland became dysfunctional, insiders say. Sutherland's name cannot be found in the index of Browne's book even though he was Chairman for most of Browne's tenure. David Simon, who was only in the job for a short time, receives high praise.

In the summer of 2006, Browne and Sutherland did manage to reach a compromise that was announced at a packed, much-anticipated press conference at BP's headquarters on July 25. Browne would stay until the end of 2008, allowing him to preside over BP's centenary year. "At the end of 2008, I will have been CEO of BP for over 13 years and that will be quite a long time," Browne said. Browne told reporters that he and Sutherland had "a good and vigorous give and take" about BP before reaching the decision on Browne's eventual departure.

As it turned out, Browne didn't last anywhere near that long. He was with friends in Barbados in early January 2007 when a reporter from the *Mail on Sunday*, a London tabloid, called a BP press officer and told him the newspaper was planning to run a story about Browne's relationship with a young Canadian, Jeff Chevalier.

Browne reacted by retaining a law firm to block publication, a move that he now says was a mistake. In his book Browne attributes his instinct to try to hide his relationship on long years of fear that his being gay would damage his career. He grew up at a time when homosexuality was illegal and could bring a prison sentence. The law changed, but Browne says "I was certain that if people in BP had known I was gay, it would have been the end of my career."

By the time Browne met Chevalier much had changed. That Browne was gay and had a boyfriend was well known in the upper reaches of BP and in elite London circles. While he lived with Browne, Chevalier was treated by BP officials as the boss's spouse, with a BP staffer even helping him with paperwork to set up an unsuccessful mobile phone ringtone business. The pair visited the homes of colleagues. Browne bought the younger man clothes, took him to receptions, and had him dine with luminaries, including Prime Minister Tony Blair.

According to an article in the *Mail on Sunday*, which exposed the Chevalier story, the young Canadian was "flaunted before business and political contacts, diplomats and artists; there were holidays in private compounds in Barbados and opera in Salzburg and Venice as guests of Prince and Princess Michael of Kent in their private box. In Venice, Mr. Chevalier found himself clinking glasses with Elton John and Jude Law."

The perks were stupendous, but Chevalier felt trapped. Browne took him to Milan and chose his clothes for him. Even the guest lists for Chevalier's birthday parties were dictated by Lord Browne and his staff. "Virtually every aspect of my life was managed by other people," he says now. "I was unable to opt out of many functions and was told I simply had to go. When I started to try to put my foot down in 2005 over which functions I attended and did not attend—to no avail—it was then I felt like a puppet."

Browne eventually ended the relationship, staking Chevalier to a year's lease on an apartment in Toronto. When Browne cut him off financially, Chevalier responded in late 2006 with what Browne calls a "carefully crafted e-mail" to the BP CEO, saying he was "facing hunger and homelessness" and asking for help. When Browne didn't respond, Chevalier went to the *Mail* with his story.

Browne's lawyers prevailed in their first effort to block publication but his career at BP was all but over. In January, the board agreed that he should be replaced by Tony Hayward in the summer.

What he hadn't told the board was that in a court document he had misrepresented the way in which he had met Chevalier. He said that it was while exercising in Battersea Park near his Chelsea home, a story that the two had used when they were a couple. Instead, newspapers reported, it was through an escort website called "Suited and Booted." Browne corrected the error later and apologized, but the damage was done. The *Mail* appealed and, on May 1, a High Court judge ruled for the paper. The false statement apparently weighed heavily in his decision. He condemned Browne's untruth, saying it is "relevant in assessing his credibility and overall merits." Mr. Justice Eady said the misstatement undercut Browne's efforts to show that Chevalier was unreliable and dependent on drugs and alcohol. He also said that he didn't see any point referring the matter for prosecution, concluding that the damage to his reputation was punishment enough, a point echoed by Browne. "I might have been 'most admired' for years but all of that was overshadowed by a momentary slip," he writes.

On the day when the judgment was announced, Browne and Sutherland concluded that he needed to resign immediately. That evening he walked out the front door of BP's headquarters on St. James Square through the scrum of journalists gathered there and into a waiting car. "It was intrusive and unpleasant," he wrote.

Browne now admits he stayed on too long. "When determination and enthusiasm turn into obsession, you lose your balance," he says. BP's board also merits criticism for not realizing that circumstances had changed. BP was under fire on several fronts, and the CEO's behavior, resisting scheduled retirement and otherwise, was showing signs of becoming an increasing risk to BP.

"For far too long BP's board failed to notice that the responses of its former CEO, Lord Browne, to massive environmental and safety disasters as well as to market-manipulation scandals did not jibe with BP's widely promoted corporate principles," wrote Jeffrey Sonnenfeld, Yale University's Lester Crowne Professor of Management Practice in *BusinessWeek*.

● ● ●

Getting rid of Browne was not enough to fix the entrenched troubles at BP or to restore its reputation. Texas City, as dramatic as it was, would not alone have been enough to permanently sully BP's reputation. The company could have written it off to a fluke accident or perhaps to a rogue facility where workers weren't living up to corporate standards. Over the next four years as investigations into the causes of the explosion raised doubts about BP's corporate culture, the oil spills in Alaska and trading scandals revealed that BP's troubles were more widespread. Many experts, adversaries and employees laid the blame at the financially-focused culture that Browne had created which measured the business units individually by the profits they generated and didn't put enough value on the safe operation of a complex and dangerous enterprise.

Chapter 7

Riding the Throughput Curve

I t was on March 2, 2006, almost a year after the Texas City blast, that Browne got another call. A pipeline at the Prudhoe Bay field on Alaska's North Slope had corroded through and was leaking oil onto the tundra. About 4,800 barrels were already on the ground.

The North Slope, including Prudhoe Bay and several smaller fields, is 250 miles above the Arctic Circle and 1,200 miles south of the North Pole. BP began developing its first field there in 1969, and it estimates its Alaska leases originally held 42.3 billion barrels of oil in place. BP, along with several oil majors including ConocoPhillips, ExxonMobil, and Chevron, produced 25 percent of U.S. crude oil on the North Slope at its peak.

The wells are serviced by a spider web-like network of pipelines and pumping stations that transport the oil from its reservoirs underground to the massive Trans Alaska Pipeline, known as TAPS. The 800-mile, four-foot-diameter pipe runs from the lower edge of the Prudhoe Bay field, across two mountain ranges, and over 800 rivers and streams, south to Valdez where tankers can bring the oil to west coast refineries. It is raised above ground to prevent the hydrocarbons from melting the frozen tundra and occasionally dips underground to ensure safe crossing points for Alaska wildlife such as caribou, wolves, and polar bears. The pipeline took three years and $8 billion to build and when it was completed in 1977 it was the most expensive and most important public works project in the United States.

BP is the operator of those smaller transit lines that lead into TAPS. TAPS itself is owned by Alyeska Pipeline Service Co., a consortium of oil companies that is 47 percent owned by BP.

The oil spill discovered at Prudhoe Bay on March 2, 2006, was, in itself, not a game-changing event. The oil sullied about two acres of tundra and most of it was cleaned up within weeks. Browne ordered his workers to "overreact" in cleaning up the mess. The leak "was bad not only for the environment but also for the company's reputation," he wrote.

He had no idea at the time how bad it would be.

Five months later, another, smaller leak was found. BP claimed that the corrosion happened suddenly and with no forewarning. But because the field was so important to the U.S. fuel supply, and because there had been earlier problems in the Trans Alaska Pipeline, the House Energy and Commerce Committee began asking questions.

What they found was that BP hadn't kept up maintenance on the pipeline network, corrosion was rampant, and the company couldn't perform the tests to find out exactly how bad it was. BP feared that the "pigs" that would run through the pipes to scrape them clean and then test their integrity would instead dislodge so much accumulated sludge that the pipes would clog and burst. Without the tests, BP had no idea where the next leak might happen. They responded by partially shutting down the field.

John Harris, Alaska's Speaker of the House at the time, wrote to Browne that he and his colleagues were "disheartened, disgusted, and downright angry" at BP for allowing the pipeline system to degrade. He accused the company's Alaska executives of lying to state officials. "We need and want a significant change in attitude, actions, account- ability and direction."

The role was a reversal for BP, which 15 years earlier had been the White Knight in Alaska after problems at the Trans Alaska Pipeline were laid at the feet of Alyeska's then-operator Exxon. Whistleblowers had reported to Congress that the pipeline was in disrepair because of negligence by the oil giant. Exxon (now ExxonMobil) and Alyeska responded by hiring security firm Wackenhut to spy on the whistle- blowers; many were subsequently fired. After damning Congressional hearings in 1993, BP took over operations at Alyeska, installing Bob Malone as CEO and investing millions to repair the aging pipes.

By the end of that decade, however, oil prices had collapsed and Prudhoe Bay wasn't pumping as much oil as it once had. Money was tight and the Alaska system, like Texas City, was being asked to do more with less.

●●●

In the oil industry, profits are shackled to the global price of oil, a price over which BP, ExxonMobil, and the other major producers have almost no control. When prices are low, as they were in the late 1990s, choosing to invest in maintenance, repairs, and upkeep can be hard to justify. How do you measure the economic benefit of safe operations? How do you put a dollar value on the absence of catastrophe?

In late 2006, BP officials denied to the House Energy Committee that cost was a factor in the pipeline's woes. But the following spring Bob Malone, who had been transferred from Alyeska to become presi- dent of BP America to help fix the newest mess on the North Slope, informed committee staffers that he had discovered thousands of pages of company records that had been withheld from lawmakers for the earlier hearing. The records showed heavy cost cutting lead the company to forego standard maintenance of the pipelines.

The Energy Committee held a hearing in May, just two weeks after Browne resigned and Hayward took over. They released dozens of internal budget documents and e-mails that showed BP had chosen to eliminate anti-corrosion chemicals in its Alaska pipeline network to meet budget goals. The e-mails and spreadsheets were eerily similar to the ones that Brent Coon revealed in his litigation over Texas City.

"They were cutting budgets and everything else up there," said Bart Stupak, a Michigan Democrat who led the investigation. "The North Slope is our most strategic energy source. They were supposed to be cleaning it out, pigging it out. Instead they skipped all that."

The documents showed that in 1999 the pipeline operators were ordered to cut costs by 10 percent. One of the decisions was to eliminate chemicals that inhibit corrosion. The internal e-mails show managers of the pipeline knew the decision would lead to degradation of the pipes.

The decision "will shorten the life of the system, resulting in either abandonment or expensive repair/replacement in the medium to long term (3 years+). The longer the corrosion continues at an uncontrolled rate, the harder it will be to arrest it and achieve satisfactory life of the equipment."

Workers were also overworked and unable to keep up with the backlog of maintenance, the documents showed. One contractor complained to BP that "our crews worked hard and made many personal sacrifices to try to meet your goals. Now, they're tired. They haven't had raises in years. There aren't enough people to do the demanded work load. They are frustrated because they can't get everything done, frustrated because they can't meet their own expectations for a high quality of thorough work."

BP that year earned $5 billion in profits. Additional budget pressure in 2002 led the company to again cut the use of corrosion inhibitors. That year, profit was $6.8 billion.

Bob Malone, who was testifying under oath in the May 2007 hearing, was asked if cost cutting could have led to the problems. "Mr. Chairman, not only could, we believe it did," Malone said. Malone agreed to appoint an outside ombudsman so workers could take their complaints to a neutral party. He chose Judge Stanley Sporkin, a federal jurist who oversaw the Alyeska spying case.

While BP as a whole was profitable in those years, the cost pressures on the North Slope were real. Oil production in the fields, which had been worked for three decades, was declining rapidly. Output was 75 percent lower than at its peak. And oil prices had plummeted from about $25 a barrel in 1996 to an average of about $15 through 1998 and 1999 before recovering again. BP knew how to maintain the pipeline network as if it were a Cadillac. Unfortunately, its value at that time was more akin to a Chevy compact.

BP, in industry parlance, was "riding the throughput curve" in trying to match costs for maintenance of the huge and expensive Alaska infrastructure to the value of the output there. In Browne's entrepreneurial management style, each business unit had to work toward its own profitability. If Alaska was losing money, the profit of the overall company was beside the point.

Even though the cost cutting had begun eight years earlier, Hayward in 2007 was the one who had to deal with the fallout. The revelation of the budget documents, and the fact that BP's own managers discussed the repercussions of their actions, and went ahead with them anyway, angered lawmakers and Alaska residents and galvanized an already active network of whistleblowers who continue to stay in constant touch with the Justice Department, Congressional investigators, and regulators.

The problems were entirely foreseeable, said Norm Szydlowski, who has run pipeline companies and Chevron's refining business. "We used to say, 'today's investment is tomorrow's reliability,'" Szydlowski, who is now CEO of SemGroup Corp., an oil and gas transporter. "If you're not spending as much or working as hard or doing the kind of maintenance you should be doing today, it's pretty certain that the problems won't show up right away, but they will show up."

● ● ●

BP's troubles may have taken Congress and the public by surprise, but its industry partners were not nearly as shocked. For instance, the buyers of two old BP fields in the North Sea, Forties and Montrose, found them in much worse condition than they expected, according to industry sources. The terrible maintenance of the Alaska pipeline record was a huge blow to the company's reputation within the oil industry, said Sadad I. Al-Husseini, a former head of exploration and production at Saudi Aramco.

Executives and board members from other majors say that BP is rarely their preferred partner in pipeline or drilling operations. Companies think that the outsourcing started by Browne during the low oil price era of the mid and late 1990s left BP unable to as closely supervise potentially risky operations as other companies do. That hasn't stopped them from doing business with the British giant, however. BP has the most leases in the Gulf of Mexico, controls the pipelines in Alaska, and has some of the best exploration abilities in the world. Many companies work with them.

Still, the reasons for BP's repeated failures in safety, maintenance, and environmental standards are more complicated than simply cutting costs. Maintaining a high-quality, well run, and safe industrial operation is as much a matter of corporate culture and incentives as it is about spending cash.

BP's culture encouraged individuals to take responsibility for their own operations rather than dictating behaviors from the top. It also incentivized things that could be measured. Worker productivity was measured in terms of financial return and safety was measured in terms of incidents. That led the company to push people to do more with less, while believing they were safe because they had few on-the-job injuries to report to the Labor Department's Occupational Safety and Health Administration, or OSHA.

In industrial organizations, there are two distinct types of safety: individual safety and process safety. A factory, ship, or refinery can excel at one while simultaneously failing at the other. Logging few worker injuries, while commendable, has little bearing on whether a major disaster is brewing. In airlines, for example, ensuring that baggage handlers don't injure their backs will do nothing to prevent an airplane from falling from the sky.

In oil and gas, the key to process safety is getting explosive hydrocarbons out of the ground, through the refining process, and to the consumer without them spilling or blowing up. Requiring refinery workers to wear hard hats and goggles won't prevent methane from escaping through a faulty valve.

BP, under Browne and again under Hayward, spent a lot of time and energy working to prevent the kinds of injuries that come from slips, trips, and falls. Company executives knew what they needed to do. They sought help in the early part of the decade from Bob Bea, director of the Center for Catastrophic Risk Management at UC Berkeley, on how to overhaul their safety regime. After the Texas City explosion, internal and external investigations showed the company was lax when it came to ensuring that the overall refining complex was run safely, and recommended changes that would help set a stronger safety culture from top to bottom. BP's leaders either didn't follow through, or they tried and failed.

● ● ●

It was 2001 when Bob Bea heard from John Browne. Browne was still basking in the success of having conquered the U.S. market with his acquisitions of Amoco and Arco. The company had earned $12 billion in profits the previous year. But there were complications.

Bea and his research partner Karlene Roberts traveled to London to meet with a group of BP executives. The integration of the new companies wasn't going well. They wanted Bea and Roberts to look around and advise them on how to proceed.

As Bea recalls it, a group of executives sat around a massive conference table in the company's headquarters, where they complained of a "clash of corporate cultures" between the new BP executives in Houston and the Amoco and Arco leaders who had remained after the mergers. "Those damn Texans won't do what we want them to do," Bea recalls one person in the room complaining.

BP had brought in senior management to train the Americans on how BP does business, Bea says. Amoco's practices were no longer relevant. It was BP's way, or the highway. They even asked the Amoco and Arco leaders to sign forms agreeing to adopt the BP way, Bea says they told him. "You're screwed," Bea told the gathering.

As a Texan, he bristled just listening to the Brits describe their attitude. "You can't go and erase the history of a company and the experience of its people simply by making them sign a little piece of paper."

In addition to trying to alter the behavior of an entire company with the stroke of a pen, Browne had set about "right-sizing" the new company, meaning cutting the workforce to match the production. BP forced much of the Amoco senior management into early retirement. Again, Bea said, "You're screwed. You just early-retired your memory. You early-retired the people who remember all those mistakes you've ever made, and you've left all the bright young people without adequate mentors."

Bea and Roberts traveled to about a dozen BP facilities—the company called them "profit centers"—including refineries in Texas, California, and Ohio. They talked to workers and managers and watched how the places were run. They found that Browne's concerns were correct. Amoco and Arco workers hadn't bought in to BP's way of doing business; morale was low and the most experienced managers were gone. The company, like many in the late 1990s, was diving headlong into the newest business fads; downsizing, outsourcing, and lean engineering. The practices, widely accepted today, can help streamline a business, allowing it to focus on what it does best and doing that more efficiently than before.

BP, Bea says, was too enthusiastic, leaving itself with a "brittle organization." "When you put them under stress they tend to collapse," Bea says. The company got rid of what seemed like redundant employees, a move generally applauded by management gurus. However, in a refinery or on an offshore rig, where the work is 24/7 and the result of a problem can be catastrophic, keeping backup in place is important. The personnel reductions "stripped away the robustness. BP became defect intolerant," Bea says. "The problem is, life is full of defects."

Carolyn Merritt, head of the Chemical Safety Board when it investigated the Texas City explosion, said at the time that the company didn't do any risk assessment of its cuts. "They had initiated cost cutting that was implemented without any review of the effect that cost cutting was going to have. You can downsize people and eliminate positions you think were unnecessary. But if you are not looking at the impact the loss of those people is going to have on overall operational safety, then you have masked a huge risk." Merritt, who died in 2008, said at the time that BP was suffering a "Culture of Denial. . . . That needs to be changed if future accidents are to be prevented."

The product of Bea's and Roberts' labors is BP's "Refining and Pipeline Leadership Fieldbook," an attractive sky-blue and orange binder that lays out a set of systems and processes that all employees should follow to run a safe ship. Inside its snap-closed cover is the motto, "Individual Brilliance/Collective Strength. Refining a great place to work." The book sits at every refinery and oil platform at BP—unopened, Bea jokes.

"They trained their refinery guys in the language of the book and then told them 'It's up to you to implement this in each refinery,'" Roberts said. "But, you have to do this within your budget, and by the way we're cutting your budget."

"Training someone is not the same as implementing things," she said.

In 2005, BP safety officials attended a conference in Normandy, France, on industrial safety, where the company made a presentation about its processes as they were presented in Bea's and Robert's Fieldbook. To train their workers throughout the world, the company hired a troupe of actors who presented the fundamentals in a comedy. "They'd taken something that's really deadly serious and made a skit out of it. They thought if their employees attended a play and read a pretty book, they'd be safe," Bea says.

Changing the behavior of an entire corporation takes much more commitment.

● ● ●

Two decades earlier Exxon embarked on a similar odyssey after the Valdez oil tanker ran aground in Prince William Sound, dumping its entire payload into the water and onto the shores of Alaska. "That accident was the low point in ExxonMobil's history. But it was also a turning point," Rex Tillerson, the company's chairman, said.

Exxon gathered a group of engineers and managers from all its units and essentially locked them in a conference room for months until they came out with a new system of safety processes that could be standardized and deployed throughout the company. The basis of the system—which contains 11 "elements"—is that it's supposed to work the same way throughout Exxon, so a roustabout could move from rig to rig and find the same safety systems and practices in place, and that safe behavior was rewarded just as productivity is.

Exxon, now ExxonMobil, deploys a risk matrix that plots every action on a graph to measure the likelihood of the event happening, and the consequences if it does. High consequence, high likelihood events show up in the upper left of the matrix. As an activity such as drilling a volatile well or cutting the costs of maintenance travels upward and leftward on the matrix, the decision has to go to higher levels of management for approval. In 2007 Exxon abandoned an ultra-deep well, known as Blackbeard, 32,000 feet below the sea floor, after spending 18 months and nearly $200 million drilling to within 2,000 feet of the planned depth. The company was panned for being too cautious for walking away from a field that was believed to have more than a billion barrels of oil. *BusinessWeek* ran an article asking whether the oil giant was "a Juggernaut or a Dinosaur."

ExxonMobil's safety matrix required them to walk away because the extreme temperatures, pressure, and complications in drilling moved the assessments inexorably upward and leftward on the risk matrix—suggesting a blowout, by definition a high consequence event, was becoming a higher and higher probability. The drillers on the rig went to their managers and said they couldn't continue. Walking away from the massive investment of time and money was a decision that went all the way to the top. Tillerson backed the drillers.

"When you have someone who's willing to put their hand up and say, 'Hey boss, I can't do it,' it sends a powerful message to the organization," says Glenn Murray, ExxonMobil's head of safety. "It tells us the system is working."

ExxonMobil's safety system means the company has backups for most technical and human systems built into its everyday operations. Changes in plans take time because risk assessments need to be done and approvals sought. Even cost-cutting proposals—such as eliminating positions or deferring maintenance—would go through a risk assessment before approval. Exxon's contractors, such as Transocean or Halliburton, have to agree to meet all of Exxon's requirements or they won't win the contract. Exxon managers are evaluated in part on how many contractors they've disqualified because they don't meet safety standards. "I can assure you it costs a lot of money," Murray says. "We've never performed a cost benefit analysis. We see it as our license to operate."

William Reilly, the EPA administrator under Ronald Reagan who, with the attorney general, fined Exxon $1 billion for the Valdez spill, said the company has made a complete turnaround. "When I talk to oil companies they all say they hate working with ExxonMobil because they're terribly rigid. It's my way or the highway with Exxon. But," Reilly pauses, "they're the best. They all say they're the best."

● ● ●

BP in 2005, and again in 2006, faced a similar turning point to Exxon's Valdez moment. The company, however, didn't succeed in turning its culture around. Changing an organization's entrenched behaviors takes a full commitment from the top. When Hayward took over, he said he would target safety with "laser-like" focus. Still, as a leader who spent years under the tutelage of John Browne, he too sent mixed messages. Just a few months after he took over, he held a town meeting at the company's Houston office where he said BP was becoming overcautious.

"I don't think having all these layers of assurance reduces risk and it can actually increase it," Hayward said, according to notes taken by an employee who was there. "The best way to reduce risk is to have deep technical competence where we need it. Individuals need to be accountable for risk and to manage it." It was a sentiment that matched the overall culture of BP, where managers were accountable for their own operations and had to live up to independent performance contracts. Creating rigid, companywide systems was anathema to BP's loose style.

One of the challenges of institutionalizing safe operations is that safety is difficult to measure. There's no obvious financial return for the expenditures. There's little to count and put on a performance evaluation. Only when something goes wrong does the return on the investment, or lack of it, become clear.

Exxon's evolution took years to achieve and was successful because of a total commitment by the company's top executives. The company used its risk matrix to protect safe operations from the cost-cutting knife. Any change, including cutting jobs or deferring maintenance, which moved the operation too far up and to the left couldn't happen.

In heavy industry, from airlines to shipping to oil and gas to astronautics, companies invest time and money investigating disasters across the world to understand what went wrong. The "lessons learned" are then supposed to be compared to their own operations to see if changes are necessary. Bea spent 20 years at Shell, and later as an independent consultant, studying disasters ranging from Unocal's 1969 Santa Barbara oil spill, to Occidental Petroleum's 1988 explosion of the Piper Alpha rig in the North Sea. He also examined the explosion of the space shuttle Columbia and the sinking of a Naval radar platform off the coast of New York.

Companies and industry groups share the findings of their investigations, and independent and quasi-governmental groups—including the Chemical Safety Board—also distribute their conclusions.

Merritt, of the Chemical Safety Board said at the time that she saw little evidence that BP truly internalized such "lessons learned," even from its own previous accidents and investigations.

In 2000, BP had three serious safety incidents, including a major fire, at its Grangemouth, Scotland refinery. The company's own report said that cost cutting played a role in the problems "There was too much focus on short-term cost reduction reinforced by key performance indicators in performance contracts, and not enough focus on longer-term investment for the future," the report said. "The safety culture tolerated this state of affairs and did not 'walk the talk.'"

BP's report on the Grangemouth problems concluded that the company's culture was not adequately focused on process safety, and that it needed an overhaul from the top, and throughout the entire operation. That never happened, according to both the Chemical Safety Board and the Baker Panel, who each concluded that the problems that led to the Texas City explosion were nearly identical to those that were found at Grangemouth.

After Texas City and Alaska, Browne ceded control of BP to Hayward. The new leader was committed to fixing the troubles at BP. He understood that explosions and spills weren't good for the company's reputation or its bottom line. His critics, however, say he didn't fully grasp the fundamental change needed to make BP consistently run a safe operation. Hayward, according to people who dealt with him in those years, continued to confound individual safety with running a safe operation. BP became obsessed with individual safety, focusing again on preventing "slips, trips and falls," Roberts says. Meetings in the headquarters often began with a "safety moment" when an attendee had to describe a recent safety incident from their life—perhaps a near car crash, or a spilled hot drink—and describe the lessons learned. One former executive recalls that walking down stairs in the company headquarters while carrying a cup of coffee was strictly banned.

BP's refinery and rig managers focused on statistics such as the number of days without injury, or the number of workdays lost due to injuries. In fact, on the day of the explosion at Texas City, several workers were enjoying a lunch provided by the company as a reward for a long string of days with no injuries reported. And on the Deepwater Horizon, an entourage of high-level BP and Transocean executives were visiting on April 20 in part to acknowledge the rig's seven years with no lost work time due to on-the-job injuries.

Focusing on those measures masked larger problems, however. Texas City's workers were aware of the pervasive safety problems at the plant and were worried. Management knew, too. In January 2005, just two months before the explosion, plant managers received an internal report that showed workers were stretched too thin, maintenance was being deferred, and morale was low. Investigators from The Telos Group interviewed hundreds of employees and in their 56-page report, they simply collated quotes from those interviews and let them speak for themselves.

We need to ensure that we have the right amount of time to complete the assigned work; we are often given a block of things that we are to complete during the day and you have to make decisions about where you can cut corners to get it all done.

We defer a lot of routine maintenance and this increases the job hazards.

We've got a lot of policies/procedures, but we compromise too much.

We need to learn from our mistakes; our organizational memory is very short; we seem to mourn for short periods of time and then move back to doing what we have always done and no meaningful changes occur from the incidents we have.

We are cut too thin.

●　●　●

Because of Texas City and Alaska, and a series of smaller infractions, congressional investigators, the Labor Department, and the Justice Department have constantly monitored BP refineries and pipelines. The company paid a $50 million criminal fine for the Texas City disaster, and another $12 million for Alaska. It remained on criminal probation when the Deepwater Horizon exploded. OSHA, in 2010, fined the company another $50 million for failing to fix the problems at Texas City, one of the conditions of its probation. Some of BP's problems could be laid at the fact that it's a bigger operator than almost any other company. It has more leases in the Gulf of Mexico. It operates the Alaska pipelines while its partners are merely passive investors, free riders as it were. Still, BP's safety violations far outstrip its rivals' and several industry officials and investigators say the company's record can't be justified by its size. OSHA cited BP for 760 "egregious and willful" violations of worker safety between June 2007 and February 2010. The company accounted for 97 percent of all willful violation citations from OSHA in that period, according to the Center for Public Integrity. The next worst offender was Sunoco, which had eight.

In the 18 months before the Horizon disaster, BP executives had been to Washington, D.C. to meet with staff members from the Energy committee at least five times to discuss safety and maintenance. Stupak says he doesn't have such a close and constant relationship with any other company.

When Henry Waxman took over as chairman of the panel in early 2009, staffers warned him that it was important to keep a close eye on BP. At about the same time, Hayward named Lamar McKay to replace Bob Malone as Chairman and President of BP America Inc. The two men traveled to Washington for an introductory meeting with Energy Committee members and staff. Malone, over his tenure, had won the respect of Congress and regulators because they saw him as forthright about BP's problems and committed to fixing them. He was always available to congressional staffers, to whom he gave the numbers to his cell and home phones. He knew how to operate in Washington, and politicians liked and trusted him. When McKay visited, he only reluctantly divulged a cell phone number, one staffer recalls.

In January 2010, just four months before the Horizon blew up, Waxman and Stupak wrote an eight-page letter to the head of BP Alaska detailing ongoing maintenance problems there. The letter listed five events in the previous 18 months, including an explosion that sent 14-foot and 28-foot lengths of pipe flying through the air to land 900 feet away, and another where a remote camera was pointed in the wrong direction, leaving workers unaware that a flare wasn't working. Combustible gas had been venting into the air for no-one-knew how long. In addition to the equipment problems, two BP contract workers on the North Slope were crushed by their own vehicles, and one died.

"If you begin to connect all those dots, you don't get a very good picture of an operator or an executive management that was looking at these high risk factors for a catastrophic incident," said Merritt.

No one in the oil industry thinks BP is incapable of running a good refinery, pipeline, or oil rig. Industry officials say they are always at the cutting edge of exploration and drilling, and are second to none at finding new oil and gas. Congressional investigators who spend their days scolding the company for accidents or pollution acknowledge they're impressed by what the company has accomplished. "Whenever they come in here, I'm just in awe of what they can do," says one. "BP does things no one else wants to do. They go places no one else wants to go," says another. "They look at me and think I'm just a bureaucrat, while they're out there facing danger. And they're right."

Still, the best engineering can be undone by poor management decision-making and complacency. In oil and gas, as one official says, "things do go boom in the night."

Chapter 8

Tony Hayward Comes Up Short

W hen John Browne abruptly resigned as chief executive of BP on May 1, 2007, the giant energy producer was struggling with a legacy of accidents and spills in the United States. Morale inside the company and among investors had flagged as its shares—once among the hottest in the oil and gas industry—were losing ground to rivals. The job of fixing BP's problems fell to Tony Hayward, Browne's successor and a 25-year veteran of the company

Hayward was chosen by the board and, specifically, by Chairman Peter Sutherland as the best of four internal candidates. They were Hayward, his deputy Andy Inglis, refining and marketing chief John Manzoni, and the current refining and marketing head, Iain Conn. Robert Dudley, a former BP executive then heading the TNK-BP, Russian subsidiary, also got a serious look from the board.

Of the five, Hayward wasn't a hard choice. Dudley, the strongest rival to Hayward, was needed to try to keep the headstrong Russian partners under control. TNK-BP was hugely important to BP, accounting for about a quarter of its production and reserves. Manzoni, whom Browne had rated highly at one point, was hopelessly tainted by the Texas City disaster and would eventually leave the company to become CEO of Talisman Energy, a mid-sized Canadian oil producer. Conn, then 44, was easily dismissed as not ready.

While the entire group was considered intelligent and hard-working, they hardly presented a diverse choice for the board. All, for instance, were men of early middle-age. All had worked at one time or other as one of Browne's executive assistants. An institution peculiar to BP, these young men, and very occasionally women, were known as "turtles," for the Teenage Mutant Ninja Turtles cartoon heroes. Browne tapped them as rising stars, and in this way he exerted almost total control over who would be given a shot at succeeding him. The turtles served in pairs and were always at Browne's beck and call. Their duties included everything from making sure his many business trips went smoothly to carrying his cigar case. All of the CEO candidates except Dudley—an American who grew up in Mississippi—were Britons, and Dudley, who had an earlier career at Amoco, was also the only one who wasn't almost a surrogate son of Browne.

Hayward had headed exploration and production, the soul and main profit center of BP since 2003. He had been at Browne's side negotiating with the likes of Russia's Vladimir Putin over BP's investment in TNK and played a role in the Amoco and ARCO transactions. Sutherland thought Hayward had picked up enough strategic vision for a successor to Browne. Hayward was more collegial than the imperious Sun King, and the board thought the publicity shy geologist would serve as a welcome antidote to Browne's flamboyance. "The board wanted him to stay out of the spotlight," says one executive. "They had had enough of that with John."

● ● ●

Hayward's awkwardness with the media and his overall lack of sophistication and seasoning cut both ways. When severely tested by the oil spill, he did not prove up to the task. When a serious crisis came, Robert Dudley, an American who had spent five years tussling with BP's powerful Russian partners, proved the far surer pair of hands.

Hayward received high marks from people who did business with him. Martin Lovegrove, Vice Chairman for Oil and Gas at Standard Chartered Bank in London and a Hayward friend says, "Tony is regarded as a first class executive by a large number of senior business people around the world. He was doing a great job for BP. Sadly, it takes more than three years to change deep-seated cultures in a company of BP's scale, however good the CEO is. Sadly, a serious accident occurred on his watch and, honorably, he took the 'silver bullet.'"

When Hayward spoke of Browne early on he did so with respect. "John has been an outstanding leader. For those of us who have had the privilege to work closely with him, he has been both a guide and an inspiration. In resigning, he placed the company ahead of himself, an act that epitomizes John's feelings for BP."

Nevertheless, the circumstances surrounding Browne's departure gave Hayward freedom to do things his own way. Hayward set a style that was the antithesis of Browne's. Browne was a natty dresser and aesthete, who remained aloof from most BP employees outside a small coterie of advisors. Hayward, the eldest of seven children, preferred soccer and Eric Clapton, he liked sailing and skiing, and was close to his son and daughter, Kieran and Tara. In his early days as CEO he would go for coffee to the employees' cafeteria in the basement of the St. James Square headquarters. Tieless and in shirtsleeves, he would meet visitors there.

Curly-haired and, like Browne, small-framed, Hayward gave straightforward answers to questions. In a July 2007 interview he said he had already visited each of BP's U.S. refineries, a troubled area for the company. During these visits he spent a full day walking around and talking to employees. Hayward was trying to create a cultural shift away from the top down management that had prevailed in the latter years of Browne's regime. Hayward believed, he said, that people on the front lines at refineries, on oil platforms—not at headquarters—had the best ideas for improving performance, a conclusion that led to a brutal cleanout of staff. "We weren't listening to the operating people on safety and reliability," he said in 2008.

Hayward and the board believed that Browne's acquisitions had outrun management's ability to integrate them. "You had an extraordinary rollup over a 15-year period," says one top BP decision maker. "John Browne was a grand acquisitor, not an effective operator. It was left to Tony and his team to restore operational discipline."

During his 25 years at BP, Hayward had established a track record as an executive who didn't mind getting his hands dirty. He joined BP in 1982 after earning at doctorate in geology from Edinburgh University, and made his first big score for the company by helping to find the Miller oil field in the North Sea on Christmas day of that year. Hayward was working on a rig at the time. Browne offered him the job of turtle or personal assistant in 1990. Hayward has said that before taking that role his knowledge had largely been limited to geology. Under Browne's tutelage he learned business, he says.

Later Hayward ran BP's Venezuelan business, which has recently been sold. He told one interviewer that the importance of safety came home to him in the Latin American nation, when he was attending the funeral of a worker killed in an accident at a BP plant and was confronted by the dead man's distraught mother.

Perhaps the most independent-minded of Browne's protégés, Hayward wasn't afraid to take the occasional shot at the culture created by Browne, if not at Browne himself. In late 2006, in what may have been an effort to stake out an independent position in advance of the board's decision on a new CEO, Hayward gave a critique of senior management's detachment from BP employees. "The top of the organization doesn't listen enough to what the bottom is saying," he said. He also issued a guarded warning about the dangers of excessive cost-cutting. "We have a management style that has made a virtue out of doing more for less," he said. "The mantra of more-for-less says we can get 100 percent of the task completed with 90 percent of the resources. Which in some senses is okay and might work, but it needs to be deployed with great judgment and wisdom. When it isn't, you run into trouble."

He said BP's exploration and production staff was overstretched by the sheer volume of projects that were underway. "We need to cool it," he said, though he denied that BP was over its head with projects such as Thunder Horse. "BP makes its money by living on the edge of technology and by doing big things," he said. "Everyone else can do the easy stuff."

● ● ●

Hayward started out right away fixing what he and the board thought was wrong with BP. The company was excellent at obtaining access to new oil and gas resources but fell short in operating its installations and executing its projects. The Hayward era would be about operational efficiency, not deals. The new chief set about simplifying and restructuring an organization that had grown far too complex. His model was ExxonMobil, the larger U.S. rival that lacks BP's creative flare in cutting deals with foreign governments or finding oil, but is known for the high quality of its operations and for bringing in projects on time and on budget.

Just after taking office, Hayward committed himself to three seemingly simple goals:

1. **Safety:** There can be no compromise on this and we must pay particular attention during this time of change.

2. **People:** Creating a company where everyone has a voice and is heard.
3. **Performance:** Focusing on reliable operations and delivering our major projects.

As Hayward's third anniversary at the helm approached, he was on a winning streak. Refineries in Texas City and Whiting, Indiana, which had been either shut down or operating at less than full capacity due to explosions and lesser problems, were now up and running. BP had been missing out on $2 billion per year in profits at Texas City alone. The much-delayed Thunder Horse project in the Gulf of Mexico was producing 300,000 barrels of oil and gas per year for BP and its minority partner, ExxonMobil. For the first quarter of 2010, profits more than doubled to $5.6 billion. In January, BP overtook Royal Dutch Shell in market capitalization for the first time in more than three years when its output increased by 4 percent, while Shell's declined.

There was no reason to doubt Hayward's seriousness about safety. In the wake of the Texas City accident, BP had asked former Secretary of State James A. Baker III to produce a report on safety at BP's U.S. refineries. The Baker report, published in January 2007, said the company was too fixated on injury statistics and not focused on assuring that its industrial processes themselves were safe. Hayward committed to increasing the refinery capital budget by $500 million each year for four years to fund improvements, including equipment upgrades and safety training. He started rolling out new, safer work procedures throughout the company, estimating that BP would be world class in safety in three to five years. BP's board was more than satisfied that the company had learned the lessons of Texas City.

But Hayward paired his stress on safety with a brutal cost-cutting drive that saw BP shed some 6500 jobs, about 10 percent of its workforce. Toward the end of his tenure, the message that costs had to be cut seemed to be louder than the one about safety. In February

2009, he said that "The mantra in BP today is 'Every dollar counts.'" He never admits that such pressures, even if well-intentioned, may have contributed to bad decisions such as the ones that led to the Macondo blowout.

Hayward also made an effort to clear away the unresolved matters in the United States that Browne had left him. He appointed Lamar McKay, a Louisianan, who had been a senior BP representative in Russia, as his U.S trouble shooter. On Oct. 25, 2007, McKay cut a deal with the U.S. Justice Department to settle a series of lingering complaints in an effort to put them away. BP pleaded guilty to a felony related to the Texas City explosion for failing to have adequate written procedures for maintaining the ongoing mechanical integrity of process equipment at the refinery, and for failing to inform contractors of the hazards related to their occupancy of temporary trailers in the vicinity of the refinery's isomerization unit. The company agreed to a $50 million fine and three years probation. In Alaska, BP pleaded guilty to a misdemeanor violation of the U.S. Federal Water Pollution Control Act and paid a $12 million fine. BP also admitted that it manipulated the price of propane in 2004 and agreed to $303.5 million in fines and restitution.

Hayward recognized that the United States loomed too large and important in BP's business to be managed from London as it was during nearly all of Browne's tenure. He appointed McKay Chairman and President of BP America Inc. McKay would be BP's chief representative in the United States.

But snafus and worse continued to plague BP. In 2009, the Occupational Safety & Health Administration (OSHA), a U.S. government agency that regulates the workplace, fined BP a record $84 million after determining that it hadn't fixed violations at Texas City. OSHA had already fined BP a previous record $21 million over the explosion. Regulators said that BP's dismal reputation over safety meant that it was now likely to attract unusual attention. For instance, after a worker was killed at Texas City in 2008, the U.S. Chemical

Safety Board, another regulator, launched an investigation. The panel's chairman John Bresland said that given its huge workload the panel wouldn't always launch a full-dress probe over one death. "With BP we would certainly give it a closer look," he said.

The regulators continued to pound away at BP. On Aug. 12, 2010, BP agreed to pay a $50.6 million fine to OSHA to settle some 270 outstanding violations and to an "aggressive schedule" to resolve hundreds of others with the help of outside monitors. The cost of the changes: $500 million over five years on top of the more than $1 billion that BP had already spent at Texas City.

Even that pact did not cure Texas City for good. In June 2010 the company acknowledged that some 500,000 pounds of toxic chemicals had leaked from Texas City, leaving people who live around the plant complaining of respiratory problems and other illnesses, and lawyers headed to the courthouse.

What was wrong? The consensus is that it takes time to change the culture of a company. Safety and doing things the right way were certainly talked about under Browne, but they weren't ingrained in the fabric of the company. Hayward tried to do so by implementing a new management regime called the Operations Management System designed to assure that tasks are performed consistently and with best practices throughout the organization. Senior managers, including Hayward, even attended an OMS "academy" set up with help from MIT. Especially before the spill, the board was satisfied with what Hayward did to improve safety. But he only had three years. As it turned out, it wasn't enough.

"Changing any culture in a large company is a long process," says Andrew Gould, CEO of Schlumberger, which provides technical services to all the major oil companies. "Tony had all the right intentions but not enough time."

● ● ●

What's striking about the Macondo disaster is that relatively low-level BP personnel on the rig made important decisions that cost the company many billions of dollars. They appear to have made the calls on whether or not to do certain tests, such as of the integrity of the cement in the well. The evidence smacks of a business unit that lacked clear procedures and rules of best practice. In many respects, exploration and production was the heart and soul of BP. It certainly earned most of the profits. That may have allowed the group to take a pass on the new standards being imposed on the rest of the company. Inglis had moved the headquarters of E&P to Houston and word around the company was that the group marched to its own drum, or at least to that of Inglis. Hayward didn't fully control E&P, a friend said. "BP didn't operate to the right standards in the Gulf of Mexico," says one insider. "E&P was a fortress; it had a certain swagger."

On September 29, even before formally taking the reigns from Hayward, BP's incoming CEO Robert Dudley announced the dissolution of the exploration and production division and Inglis's departure. Inglis was replaced by three people, none of whom would, as Inglis had, sit on BP's board.

After Inglis interrupted Hayward's breakfast with that terrible phone call on April 21, the CEO quickly gathered his inner circle: Chief of Staff Steve Westwell, Rupert Bondy, the group's general counsel, and Communications head Andrew Gowers. Hayward was saddened by the loss of life and shocked and angry that such an accident could have happened after all he did to try to prevent it. On the next day he flew to Houston. He remained in the United States, with brief interruptions, until the end of June.

The toll the situation was exacting on Hayward was already evident 12 days after the accident on May 2 when the CEO slipped into a booth at Copeland's, a restaurant on the main drag of Houma, the southern Louisiana town rising from the swamps and agricultural land, from which BP was mounting much of its cleanup operation. Hayward usually came across as self-confident, even cocky, but this time, dressed in a white shirt unbuttoned at the collar, his small round face had a sheen of sweat and his eyes had a haunted look. He picked at his ravioli and only sipped his beer. He joked about not remembering the details of the odyssey of the previous two weeks: Governors' mansions, Washington officials' offices, even a quick trip back to London to visit his wife, Maureen, who had undergone an operation. He kept repeating a phrase he said was coined by Winston Churchill: "When you are going through hell, keep going."

Hayward seemed stunned by the failure of a massive piece of equipment called a blowout preventer (BOP) that sits on top of the well and is intended to stop such disasters. He seemed to have complete faith in BOPs even though studies have shown them to be far from flawless. "The thing is designed to keep drilling safe," he said.

Hayward insisted that the accident was the fault of the drilling company, Transocean, not BP. "It is not our rig, not our equipment, not our systems," he told the BBC on May 3. But at dinner he seemed to be edging toward the conclusion that BP and perhaps other companies had not supervised contractors such as Transocean closely enough. "There may be a need to do more oversight of drilling equipment," he says. Then, exhausted, he drove off to where he was spending the night—a Ramada Inn undergoing a major renovation with its parking lots full of the pickup trucks of cleanup workers.

By this time, about two weeks into the spill, Hayward and BP were already in deep trouble. Hayward was determined to be the public face of BP, a decision that proved to be fatal for his career at the company. His natural cockiness, a tendency to say whatever was on his mind, and his British accent did not play well on American television. Hayward and BP repeatedly underestimated the volume of oil pouring from the stricken well, destroying their credibility with the American public. First, the company said there was no leak. Then, over the weekend of April 24, it put out estimates of "up to" 1,000 barrels per day. Eventually the government put the volume at as high as 62,000 barrels per day. While he was spending all his time trying to contain the spill and handle the fallout from it, Hayward seemed to underestimate its seriousness. He repeatedly claimed that BP had organized "a massive over-response" to the spill.

BP did mount a large and early response to the disaster. Steve Venz, CEO of the Marine Spill Response Corp., an industry-funded group, says his organization got a call from BP's crisis team at 12:09 Central time, about two hours after the explosion. MRCS, probably the largest contractor involved in the cleanup operation, quickly had four 210-foot oil-skimming ships and two planes for spraying chemicals to disperse the floating oil on the scene. They were initially unable to operate because of the fire on the platform and the search and rescue operation for the 11 crewmen who were killed. "We had more equipment within the first 48 hours than would have been required for a worst-case tanker discharge," he says.

As the oil continued to flow and the spill spread, BP assembled a small air force and navy with at least nine planes and hundreds of ships. BP's logistics base for the Gulf at Houma was turned into a command center for the operation. In a large, high-ceilinged room, uniformed coast guard personnel mingled with specialists from BP and other oil companies, such as ExxonMobil. Spill experts say the well-funded operation drew a "Who's-who" of their niche industry. One of them, Jacqueline Michel, President of Research Planning Inc., a Columbia, S.C. consulting firm, says BP "is throwing everything at the spill; there is no expense spared."

But no cleanup effort could stop the more serious problem: the ongoing outrush of oil from the well. The nerve center for the efforts to kill the well, or at least contain the leaking oil, was on the third floor of BP's exploration and production building in Houston known as Westlake 4. The heart of the operation is a room known as "the hive," where BP Gulf of Mexico explorers meet to view 3D seismic images and debate whether they reveal deposits of oil. After the blowout the hive was transformed into a center for monitoring the dozen remote operating vehicles that are working for BP at the disaster site. It is a darkened cavernous room. Technicians sat at tables watching a bank of video screens showing feeds from the undersea robots, which are painted yellow and seemed to fly about like great insects in the inky green darkness.

Hayward compared working with robots to "an Apollo 13 exercise." In the early days of the leak, Hayward watched in frustration as the robots failed to make the blowout preventer work. In early May, BP tried to lower a giant cone, four stories high, over the well to contain the oil. That strategy also failed, when natural gas hitting the near freezing sub-sea water formed crystals called hydrates, which gummed up the cone.

On May 26, BP launched a much-publicized "top kill" effort, involving pumping heavy drilling mud and even golf balls down into the well. BP and the U.S. government put a lot of prestige on the line in preparing this procedure. Both Hayward and Energy Secretary Steven Chu, a Nobel-prize winner, were present at BP's headquarters in Houston, and Hayward suggested there was a 60 to 70 percent chance of success. But, after four days of differing reports about the progress of the procedure BP, was forced to abandon it.

That failure unleashed the full hostility of the Obama administration. The President termed the failure to plug the leak "as enraging as it is heartbreaking." He said: "We will not relent until the leak is contained, until the waters and shores are cleaned up, and until the people unjustly victimized by this man-made disaster are made whole."

• • •

These comments were the beginning of what may turn out to be the most dangerous period for BP and a time when Hayward took what turned out to be a fatal beating from the U.S. media and politicians.

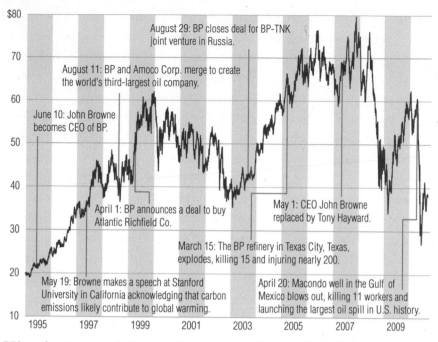

August 29: BP closes deal for BP-TNK joint venture in Russia.

August 11: BP and Amoco Corp. merge to create the world's third-largest oil company.

June 10: John Browne becomes CEO of BP.

April 1: BP announces a deal to buy Atlantic Richfield Co.

May 1: CEO John Browne replaced by Tony Hayward.

March 15: The BP refinery in Texas City, Texas, explodes, killing 15 and injuring nearly 200.

May 19: Browne makes a speech at Stanford University in California acknowledging that carbon emissions likely contribute to global warming.

April 20: Macondo well in the Gulf of Mexico blows out, killing 11 workers and launching the largest oil spill in U.S. history.

BP's stock price enjoyed a long march upward over 15 years until the Deepwater Horizon disaster and subsequent oil spill erased almost all the gains.
Source: Bloomberg News, Seth Myers.

Before April 20, Hayward had overseen a 16 percent increase in BP's stock price to $60.48 in New York trading. When it announced the top kill had failed on June 1, it fell to $36.52. The plummeting shares were wiping out the wealth of BP employees and putting pressure on the value of British pension funds, most of which were invested in the company. Analysts' estimates of the costs of the spill soared to as high as $60 billion. At the same time, the price of BP's credit default swaps, the cost of insuring its debt, soared. The company began what seemed an almost desperate attempt to raise emergency funds, going around to banks and to sovereign wealth funds. For the first time, the notion of bankruptcy emerged in analysts' comments, and, insiders say, the company's management became seriously worried.

Meanwhile Hayward picked a bad time to put his foot in his mouth. Giving reporters a beach tour of the cleanup effort on May 30, he said: "No one wants this thing over more than I do. You know I'd like my life back." With 11 people killed in the initial explosion, and several others injured, the comment came across as inexcusably insensitive. A headline in *The New York Daily News* called Hayward "the most hated—and the most clueless—man in America." Obama said on June 8 that "he wouldn't be working for me after any of those statements."

On one of his rare visits to London, on the night of June 7, Hayward gave a very strange party. A group of "friends," including Vittorio Colao, head of telecom company Vodafone PLC, Martin Sorrell, chief of advertising firm WPP PLC, Frank Chapman, CEO of gas giant BG Group, BP board members, and former and current staff gathered for drinks on the sixth floor of the company's London headquarters at Hayward's personal invitation. John Sawers, Chief of the British foreign intelligence agency, MI6, was there, possibly providing evidence of the British government's concern about the assault on one of the country's most important companies. Hayward, dressed in a checked shirt and rumpled blue suit, worked the room but did not give a briefing as expected. One CEO present remarked that he thought the occasion "bizarre."

Much in evidence was the wide gap in perception between the United States and Britain of the seriousness of the Gulf of Mexico oil spill. Many people in London business circles considered the heated U.S. reaction overdone and verging on hysteria. They attributed the ferocity of attacks on BP to the company's foreignness. One board member told another guest: "There is only oil on six beaches, but we are not allowed to say that."

Hayward's next public relations fiasco was his June 17 appearance before a congressional committee investigating the disaster. Three days before the hearing, Congressmen Henry Waxman, chairman of the Energy and Commerce committee, and Bart Stupak, head of its Subcommittee on Oversight and Investigations, detailed in a 14-page letter to Hayward what they believed were decisions made by BP engineers that led to the blowout and massive oil spill. "Time after time, it appears that BP made decisions that increased the risk of a blowout to save the company time or expense," the Congressmen wrote. "If this is what happened, BP's carelessness and complacency have inflicted a heavy toll on the Gulf, its inhabitants, and the workers on the rig."

Along with the letter, the committee released 22 internal documents, including e-mails between BP drilling engineers calling Macondo a "nightmare well" and discussing the costs of various well equipment, and finally choosing the lowest cost option. The letter was devastating to BP. It led to days of news stories repeating the congressmen's conclusion and stoked anticipation of Hayward's testimony.

The BP camp was stunned by the letter and interpreted it as evidence that BP would not receive a fair hearing from the committee. That attitude led Hayward's advisors to urge him to hunker down and give nothing away. The company believed that, like it or not, it was in for a ritual beating and that Hayward had no choice but absorb it.

Though the event was briefly enlivened when Rep. Joe Barton apologized to Hayward and BP for what he called a "shakedown" by the White House, Hayward declined to answer most questions. While lawmakers fumed, Hayward repeatedly said he didn't have firsthand knowledge of what had happened or wasn't involved in decisions. Rep. Bart Stupak, a Michigan Democrat, told Hayward he and other committee members were "extremely frustrated with your lack of, and/or inability to answer questions." Henry Waxman, the panel's chairman, described the CEO's responses as "stonewalling." "I'm not stonewalling," Hayward responded. According to a transcript of his testimony, Hayward claimed ignorance to what happened on the Deepwater Horizon, saying at least 23 times he was not involved in decisions.

The strategy was a mistake. Whatever the politicians' motives, the hearing was Hayward's opportunity to take responsibility, show remorse, and speak to the U.S. public. Instead, he enraged lawmakers and simultaneously gave the already suspicious public the impression he had something to hide.

Hayward may have been hopeless as a communicator, but his staff and other advisors, as well as the U.S. government, certainly didn't serve him well. He was repeatedly given lowball estimates of the volume of the spill, and overly optimistic forecasts of the efficacy of the various kill and containment procedures. BP also completely failed to make its case in Washington despite years of lobbying.

Once Hayward returned to Britain in June, his taking part in a boat race around the Isle of Wight on a $270,000 Farr 52 racing yacht called "Bob" that he co-owned with an investment banker named Rob Gray and Sam Laidlaw, CEO of utility Centrica, was an extraordinary lapse. Hayward's picture appeared in the newspapers the next day with his face barely peeping out from foul weather gear. Even friends were appalled, with one saying that Hayward was shell-shocked after his drubbing in the United States "I think we can all conclude that Tony Hayward is not going to have a second career in PR consulting," quipped White House Chief of Staff Rahm Emmanuel.

While this sorry spectacle played out, the BP board fumed. Meeting almost weekly by phone, the board struggled to keep up with the worsening situation. With each barrel of oil spilled, the company's financial liability rose. Throughout the summer Hayward had been sounding out friends and board members over whether he could survive. Some board members felt that his low standing in the United States and with the Obama administration meant that his ouster had to be part of a recovery scenario. Others argued that Hayward had done a good job and that continuity was valuable.

● ● ●

Ironically, what finally doomed Hayward was success in capping the well. BP managed to shut off the flow of oil with a new capping system on July 15. For some of the more activist board members, including Paul Anderson, a former BHP Billiton chief executive, that was the milestone that opened the way to replace Hayward with a new face needed to lead the company's recovery. Hayward behaved as if he had a shot at retaining his job up to the week that began on July 12. Svanberg, the Chairman, and other board members had been encouraging. But through conversations late in that week and over the weekend of July 17 to 18, Hayward recognized that he didn't have the support to continue, BP sources say. The company began preparing for his departure early in the week beginning July 19. Still, knowing that he had to go for the good of the company didn't make it easy for Hayward to accept. As events unfolded, he was emotional, even teary, at certain moments.

On July 27, the company announced that Hayward would leave and be succeeded by Dudley as of Oct. 1, 2010. The same day the company announced a record quarterly loss of $17.2 billion, after writing off the estimated costs of paying for the spill.

"It's a tragedy; he got hit by an asteroid," was how one sympathizer put it. Unlike many ousted U.S. CEOs, Hayward did not get a huge package for going away: Just the year's salary he was entitled to and his already accumulated pension. Total value: $17.2 million. A BP official said the board was determined that there would be no reward for failure.

The day his replacement was announced can not have been pleasant for Hayward. As television crews waited outside BP's St. James headquarters, Hayward sat through press conferences as a kind of third wheel with his chosen successor, Robert Dudley, and BP's suddenly active Chairman Carl-Henric Svanberg. Occasionally a streak of bitterness showed through. In a meeting with a group of reporters Hayward said that he had been "demonized and vilified" in the United States and "BP can't move on in the United States with me as its leader. It is a practical matter, not whether it is fair or not. Life is not fair."

Dudley, the Mississippian chosen to try to fix BP's United States problems, was subdued. "This is a sad day," he said. Yet he also made clear, in a drawl familiar to the Gulf Coast residents who were so angry at his company, that he could make the connection with Americans that eluded Hayward. He said his father had taught college in Hattiesburg, Mississippi, and he had spent time as a teenager on the water at Biloxi and Gulfport. "I know what it is like to jump off and swim off a boat in the Gulf. I know what crabbing, shrimping, and fishing is all about."

Hayward never made the connection.

Chapter 9

Disaster on the Horizon

H ayward's aspirations to transform BP into another ExxonMobil died on April 20 when the Deepwater Horizon exploded. The company's reputation among regulators, contractors, and its peers was already tainted because of Texas City and Prudhoe Bay. Now the conflagration in the Gulf and, later, the stream of oil flowing into the water, the blackened beaches, and oiled birds would confirm to many that BP was a bad actor.

There were at least three companies involved in the actual drilling of the Macondo well on the day the rig blew up, and the many inquiries into the causes of the disaster show there was blame and responsibility to go around. BP owned the lease and designed the well and its managers directed the rig crew on what to do and when to do it. Transocean owned the rig and its crew did the actual drilling. Halliburton, the oil services company, was responsible for cementing the well to ensure the oil and gas stayed underground and did not dangerously rise up the well.

The picture that has emerged from the investigations is one of a crew that was under immense cost and time pressure by their employers, and who, industry officials say, were speeding to finish the job. They were weeks behind schedule on a difficult well and in the end, appeared to take shortcuts to save time and money as they moved through the crucial steps of completing and sealing the well.

The operation aboard the Deepwater Horizon lacked the rigid safety procedures or discipline that would have led BP and Transocean crewmembers to ask more questions, seek advice of superiors before making decisions to alter the nature of the well, and stop the work if they were unsure the situation was stable. Workers on the rig, and managers in Houston, made a series of disastrous decisions that sealed the fate of the rig.

The lessons learned at Texas City and Prudhoe Bay apparently hadn't reached the Gulf of Mexico.

● ● ●

BP began drilling the Macondo well on October 7, 2009, using another Transocean drill rig called the Marianas, in a nine-square-mile section of the seafloor known as Mississippi Canyon 252. The well on the seabed, about 5,000 feet below the surface, was considered deepwater though not unusual. A month after drilling began, the company informed the MMS that the Marianas' blowout preventer needed repairs.

The blowout preventer (BOP) is a 50-foot-tall stack of pipes and valves designed to suppress surges of high-pressure gas and oil that can shoot up the well shaft. Most rigs have a variety of types of preventive devices stacked atop each other in the unit at the wellhead at the bottom of the sea. Some of the BOP devices close around the open space between the drill pipe and the outside of the well to prevent oil and gas from escaping through that route. Drillers will squeeze them shut if pressure from below starts pushing drilling mud up the well. Then they make the mud heavier to hold the oil back and shoot it into the well through a separate pipe called a kill line. A separate preventer, called a shear ram, is the rig's savior of last resort and is only supposed to be used in extremis. If oil or gas shoot up the well, and the rest of the safety devices can't stop it, the shear ram is supposed to slice through the well casing and drill pipe to free the rig from the well and, hopefully, pinch the pipes shut.

BP stopped the drilling at Macondo in the fall of 2009 so rig workers could fix the blowout preventer. They were still at it when Hurricane Ida churned through the Gulf during the second week of November 2009, prompting an evacuation of offshore rigs and plat-forms. When the weather cleared and the crew returned to the Marianas, they found damage to the electrical wiring under the main deck. In January, BP released the Marianas from its lease and brought in Transocean's $365 million Deepwater Horizon, which it was leasing for $510,000 a day, to finish the job that was now more than two months behind schedule.

The Deepwater Horizon arrived above Macondo and lowered a "riser," a mile-long hollow tube made of lengths of steel pipe, down to the ocean floor. The riser has a series of ball and slip joints that allow it to stay in place even as the floating rig above moves about in the water. The rig workers drill the well using a drill bit that is lowered down the riser to the seafloor at the end of a series of 90-foot-long, 600-pound, narrow steel pipes that screw together, forming what's known as the drill string. Drillers add lengths to the string from above as they drill deeper. They also include "collars," that can weigh as much as 4,000 pounds, to give the drill string stability. As the well gets deeper, rig workers stabilize its walls by periodically installing steel casings and cementing them to the outside rock walls of the well.

Just a week after the Horizon arrived at Macondo and its crew began work, BP reported to the MMS that the rock formation where it was drilling was cracking under the pressure of the equipment, and drilling mud was being lost down the hole. Left unsealed, cracks in the surrounding rock formation can allow natural gas, or toxic gas such as hydrogen sulfide, to rush up the shaft to the rig, poisoning the rig crew or blowing up the platform.

The Transocean crew on February 13, 2010, attempted a "cement squeeze," which involves pumping cement into the hole at high pressure to force it into the fissures and seal them. "Most of the time you do a squeeze and then let it dry and you're done," says John Wang, an assistant professor of petroleum and natural gas engineering a Penn State in University Park, Pennsylvania. "It dries within a few hours."

This time was different. It took 10 days and about eight tries, using substances with names like Form-A-Squeeze and Form-A-Set, before logs filed with the MMS show the well was "static" or stable.

The problems didn't lead the crew to proceed with more caution, however. BP officials on the Horizon, known as "company men," made it clear to the Transocean drillers that they were in a rush to finish this job. "It was just passed around via people that this well was taking too long and that they were in a hurry to complete it so they could move on to the next," said Douglas Brown, the Horizon's chief mechanic. BP wanted to move the rig east to a subsea tract known as Viosca Knoll, to commence work on another project, according to a permit application the oil company filed with the minerals agency. BP's plan called for work to begin on Viosca Knoll with the Deepwater Horizon starting on March 8, which meant it was already 43 days behind schedule when the disaster struck the Macondo well. The plan in place at the time of the blowout was to move the Horizon on April 27.

Jason Anderson, a Transocean "toolpusher," who died manning the drill when the rig exploded, had told his father that BP managers were in a rush and pushing the crew to take shortcuts to get the well finished. "The last two times he was home he said they were putting more and more pressure on him and he was worried," said Billy Anderson at his home near Blessing, Texas, about 110 miles southwest of Houston.

By March 8 the company had drilled to 13,305 feet at Macondo but still had a lot of work to do. Two days later the Transocean crew encountered more problems, when gas began to surge up the well to the platform. "We're in the midst of a well control situation." BP wrote in an e-mail to Frank Patton, the mineral service's drilling engineer for the New Orleans district.

"Well control situation" is a euphemism for what can be a terrifying event. Controlling a well essentially means ensuring the hydrocarbons that were sealed under the earth don't surge uncontrollably to the surface once their tomb is punctured. In the industry, "well control" is the term used for the effort to keep the oil below the surface until they're ready to pump it out. To keep a well under control during drilling, rig workers pump a heavy slurry called "drilling mud" down a pipe that goes into the drill bit. The mud then squirts out the tip of the bit and circulates back up the sides of the well to the rig.

On the rig are mud engineers. Their titles sound mundane, but their jobs are crucial and require high skill. A mud engineer spends his time ensuring the weight of the mud puts more downward pressure on the oil than its own upward force. If the mud proves too light, he'll add a substance such as barite to add weight. He may add lubricants and other materials so the fluid allows the bit to drill smoothly, with minimal friction, so it doesn't add to the already intense heat of the oil below the surface. Anyone involved in drilling on a rig will have attended "well control" school. "Well control is part of drilling; that's what drilling operations are about," says Rex Tillerson, the CEO of ExxonMobil. "You are trying to drill into the forces of Mother Nature and hold that back in a controlled fashion until you can then secure it."

On March 10, the drillers at Macondo experienced a "kick"; this happens when the pressure from below the surface exceeds the pressure being put down the well with drilling mud. Natural gas floated up into the air surrounding the Deepwater Horizon. Rig managers ordered a stop to all "hot work"—anything involving electricity or machinery that could cause a spark and ignite the explosive fumes.

"They damn near blew up the rig," said Robert Bea, an engineering professor at the University of California, Berkeley, who consulted with BP on safety and chairs an independent group investigating the Deepwater Horizon explosion. Drilling officials managed to pump enough heavy mud into the well to contain the surging gas. Oil industry executives say the Gulf is particularly tricky to drill because the layers of salt conceal pressured pockets of gas that are hard to anticipate.

This particular snafu led to the walls of the well collapsing. The drill pipe became stuck in the well. Drillers were forced to cut the pipe, leaving $25 million worth of drilling tools in a hole at the bottom of the sea. The drillers asked MMS for permission to drill a sidetrack 100 feet to the side of the trouble spot and then loop back to the original well plan. MMS approved the 15-page drilling plan revision in 30 minutes. "These were early warnings," says Bea, who spent 20 years with Shell working offshore and designing rigs. "The formation is trying to talk to you. On the rig they call it 'listening to the well.'"

Whether BP should have continued drilling in a rock formation that was proving to be so unstable is a matter of debate. In 2005, ExxonMobil abandoned a deep well called Blackbeard after similar kicks, and was roundly panned in the macho oil industry for lacking the courage to follow through with a challenging project. *BusinessWeek* ran an article asking whether the oil giant was "a Juggernaut or a Dinosaur." After the Macondo well blew out, ExxonMobil's actions looked wise and even fashionable.

Still, the decision to stop a major job can be a career-ender, said Bea. Workers, while they technically have the right to do so, fear the repercussions if they make a decision that costs the company money for no reason.

"A good decision doesn't always lead to a good outcome," says Norm Szydlowski, CEO of SemGroup Corp. and former CEO of Colonial Pipeline Inc. "The controller in the control room shuts down a pipeline because he was uncertain about something he saw, and it turns out it was nothing. Now's the moment of truth. Will the boss say, 'good decision' or will he say 'that was dumber than dirt.'"

●   ●   ●

Two days after the near blowout, BP began drilling again. Throughout these weeks, Transocean tested its blowout preventer several times and the drillers held frequent firefighting and abandon ship drills. Such safety practice is an integral part of life on an offshore rig, where workers understand that safe operation of the ship and the drilling equipment are a matter of life and death. The first thing you do when you get a job on an oil rig is qualify for safety. Workers usually have 30 days to learn about all the safety procedures and equipment, and every person has a responsibility in case of an emergency.

People on a rig work together in close quarters for weeks at a time. They form close bonds and their role in an emergency becomes a matter of deep personal responsibility. All it takes is for one person not to do his job, and the rig could blow up, killing everyone. Along with the responsibility comes the machismo of being a guy from Texas or Oklahoma who does hard physical labor in dangerous conditions. People respect the guy who can get things done. "Nobody wants to be the guy during the fire who drops the hose and runs," said Don Fitzgerald, a former Navy Lieutenant who also worked on offshore oil rigs.

There are only two real emergencies on an oil rig, sinking and fire. A blowout can cause either. As gas escapes from a deep sea well and rushes to the surface, it can create a huge bubble under the platform. The rig falls into the bubble and sinks. It's akin to a torpedo sinking a ship—the weapon doesn't slam into the target, it explodes beneath it creating a void that causes the ship to buckle. At Macondo, the gas didn't form a bubble, it rushed up the well and enveloped the rig with explosive vapors that ignited. Mike Williams and Stephen Stone, a roustabout, both say that the well suffered an unusually large number of kicks, leaving most of the offshore workers uneasy about Macondo. The gas surges didn't show up frequently in the weekly well activity reports submitted to the Minerals Management Service in New Orleans, a review of the documents shows. Frank Patton says he never knew about any kicks other than the one reported on March 10.

After struggling with the well for nearly 10 weeks, BP and Transocean reached the planned depth of 18,360 feet below the sea surface. BP well engineers then had to decide how to secure the well and move on.

• • •

There are few hard standards or rules for offshore drilling. Companies design their wells and create a drilling plan according to the specific geological conditions they believe they'll encounter in that particular spot. As the drilling progresses and the workers on the rig "listen to the well," the plan evolves. Decisions about what tests to run, how to interpret data such as well pressures and gas levels, and how to deal with complications in the well are left to the judgment of rig managers and engineers on shore. On the Deepwater Horizon, rig managers spoke on the phone every morning with BP's and Transocean's onshore supervisors to discuss the plan for the day.

Once the Horizon's drill reached the desired well depth of 18,360 feet, BP's engineers had a choice of whether to finish the job by running a "long-string" steel casing all the way from the sea floor to the bottom of the well, or a "liner and tie-back" from the last point at which the well was secured. The first option would cost less money and take less time and might have longer life, but could also provide less security against at blowout because there would be fewer cement barriers between the reservoir and the surface, according to Congressional investigators led by Henry Waxman of California and Bart Stupak of Michigan.

Internal documents showed BP engineers changed their minds multiple times, first preferring the long string and then rejecting it because "cement simulations indicated it's unlikely to be a successful cement job." They reversed course again two days later, on April 15, saying it would be "possible to obtain a successful cement job" and that the long string offers the "best economic case and well integrity case for future completion operations." BP engineers chose that option. MMS approved the permit that day.

"That may be an acceptable design, but not for a well that deep," said Stupak, who led the House Energy Committee's investigation into the disaster. "The farther you go down, the less integrity that well will have. If you're using that design, it requires you to take stronger precautions to make sure the integrity of that design withstands the pressures."

The choice was made to reduce time and costs, Stupak and Waxman said in a 14-page letter to Tony Hayward in June, 2010. BP disagrees. "The design is robust," says Kent Corser, BP's drilling engineering manager. "It meets all the MMS criteria and it meets all the BP criteria. We do not think that the long string had any bearing on this event." Indeed, many other wells in the Gulf of Mexico are of similar design.

BP engineers may have compromised the cement job, which prevents oil and gas from surging up the well, when they chose to use fewer so-called "centralizers" than was recommended by a Halliburton cementing consultant. The President's commission investigating the disaster concluded that the cement job failed, contributing to the blowout. Oil companies use centralizers—springy devices that surround the well pipe—to keep the drill string in the middle of the hole, making it easier to pump cement evenly to seal the empty space between the casing and the rock formation. Halliburton, BP's cementing contractor, advised the company to use 21 centralizers; BP had only six on the Horizon, so company engineers told Halliburton to design the cement work for those. Halliburton warned in an e-mail that BP was risking "severe gas flow."

Internal e-mails suggest time pressure was weighing on the engineers. BP's Well Team Leader, John Guide, said it was too late to get additional centralizers to the rig. Shortly after midnight on April 16, Gregory Walz, BP's Drilling Engineering Team Leader, e-mailed Guide to say he'd found 15 more centralizers and would fly them to the rig that morning. "There has been a lot of discussion about this and there are differing opinions on the model accuracy. However the issue is that we need to honor the modeling to be consistent with our previous decisions to go with the long string," Walz said. In the same e-mail, however, he showed immediate remorse.

"John, I do not like or want to disrupt your operations and I am a full believer that a rig needs only one team leader. I know the planning has been lagging behind the operations and I have to turn that around," Walz told Guide.

Guide, however, objected to using the new centralizers because he believed they weren't the appropriate design and because they would take an additional 10 hours to install, e-mails showed. "We are adding 45 pieces that can come off as a last minute decision. I do not like this and I [am] very concerned about using them," he said in an e-mail back to Walz. The team decided to rely on Halliburton to do a solid cement job either way. "Who cares, it's done, end of story, will probably be fine and we'll get a good cement job," one engineer said in an e-mail.

The drillers, however, never tested the well to see if that happened. On April 19, BP flew a crew from Schlumberger Ltd., an oil field services company, to the rig to test whether Halliburton's cement sealed the well or left channels where gas could escape. BP decided against running the cement test, which would have cost $128,000, and sent the Schlumberger crew home on a departing helicopter at 1:40 P.M. on April 20, just eight hours before the blowout. A well control specialist at another oil company estimates that BP's suite of decisions on Macondo would have saved the company $10 to $15 million. The decision suggests the workers were rushing to complete the well, said

Reilly, co-chair of the Oil Spill Commission. "One must ask where the drive came from that made people determine that they couldn't wait for sound cement or for the right centralizers."

CEOs from four of BP's rivals told a congressional hearing that they would have made different decisions. Rex Tillerson of ExxonMobil was particularly damning.

> We would have used a different cement formulation, we would have tested for cement integrity before we circulated the kill-weight mud out, we would have had the locking seal ring at the casing hanger before proceeding.
>
> And leading up to all of that, though, there was clearly—and this is just based on what has publicly been made available—there were clearly a lot of indications or problems with this well going on for some period of time leading up to the final loss of control. And why those—why—how those were dealt with and why they weren't dealt with differently I don't know.

● ● ●

BP's own investigators, who spent four months examining the disaster, exonerated the design of the well and, instead, pointed to a series of equipment failures and faulty crew decisions. The investigation, led by Mark Bly, the head of safety, concluded natural gas flowed up the well through the drill string at its center rather than in the spaces between the drill pipe and the casing. The President's commission agreed. That interpretation means the type of casing—long string or liner—had no role in the disaster.

Bly and government investigators relied on real-time data available from the Macondo well that shows the minute-by-minute changes in the flow of fluids, temperatures, and well pressures. Both investigations concluded that the speed of the rising pressure and arrival of hydrocarbons at the surface proved it couldn't have escaped through the well casing. Their data suggests that the cement work done by Halliburton failed.

Halliburton used cement infused with nitrogen that would make it foamy, lighter, and less likely to crack the fragile rock surrounding the well. Bly concluded that cement failed. Tests run after the fact by BP engineers using similar cement suggested that the Halliburton formula may have failed to dry properly and, instead, collapsed the way foam shaving cream will collapse if left sitting in a cup. BP and the Oil Spill Commission ran tests on similar cement that showed the Halliburton formula was unstable and in fact may have collapsed, the way foam shaving cream will collapse when left sitting in a cup. Halliburton tests run before April 20 showed the cement to be unstable, according to Commission lawyers. The contractor ran four tests—all of which had bad results—but only gave BP the results of one. "It doesn't appear that anybody highlighted this information," said Sean Grimsley, a lawyer for the Commission.

Transocean's workers were preoccupied with preparing to move the Horizon from Macondo to its next well, and missed the early signs of trouble, Bly's report said. Pressure in the well became unbalanced shortly before 9 P.M., and the well began producing prematurely. About 39 barrels of fluid surged up the pipe from the well in 10 minutes. Drilling experts say that such events are not rare, but that the rig crew needs to be paying close attention so as to be able to take action when they do.

That oil and gas were flowing up the well may have been masked because rig workers were emptying mud from the rig to a service boat to prepare for the move. "It appears the pits were not being monitored," said Steve Robinson, BP's vice president of exploration. Starting at 9:15, pressure in the drill pipe was increasing, but Transocean's workers didn't seem to notice. "We do not see any indication that there were any well control actions being taken at this point. They were not aware. They were not aware that there was a well control problem," Robinson said.

Picking up signs of problems requires extreme vigilance. To detect the beginning of the blowout, the driller on duty would have to have noticed two lines diverge on a computer screen, as the pressure from one pipe rose and the other stayed constant. Nobody knows what the driller, Dewey Revette, who was killed in the blast, saw on the screens in the drill shack that night. "A lot of this depends on the right person with the right knowledge and the right background and the right experience being at the right place at the right time and seeing the right information and making a decision quick," said Fred Bartlit, lead counsel to the Oil Spill Commission.

Gas started to envelop the rig at 9:38 when Mike Williams and his wife heard the mudlogger announce that gas levels were rising. Two minutes later mud started flowing from the drill pipe onto the floor and shooting up the derrick.

At that point, 40 long minutes after the first signs of the blowout, the Transocean drillers finally reacted. They diverted the mud to a mud/gas separator on board, where the gas was able to enter the rig's ventilation system, rather than over the side of the rig, and then they tried to close the blowout preventer. The first decision was a mistake, BP investigators say, and became fatal when the blowout preventer failed.

The mud/gas separator sent the explosive methane into the rig's ventilation system that then released it through ducts all over the Deepwater Horizon. BP models show the gas would have been released underneath the rig floor, into the air surrounding the engine room, and across the rear of the rig where living quarters were. The captain or the chief mate came over the radio to warn a nearby supply boat to back away because the rig was "in a well control situation," Brown told investigators.

That was when Mike Williams heard the engines revving faster and faster, probably the result of the highly charged gas entering the engine room through its ventilation system. Shortly thereafter, the first explosion rocked the rig.

At that point the only thing that might have saved the rig was the blowout preventer. BP's investigation concluded that the last-resort safety device hadn't been adequately maintained and failed when it was needed. The Horizon's blowout preventer, which weighed 300 tons and was as tall as a four-story building, had two annular preventers, and five rams. There were six ways to activate it, including a "dead man" that tells the shear ram to cut through the casing and drill pipe if the rig loses power and hydraulic pressure. None of these layers of protection worked on April 20. Its two underwater control pods were faulty. On the first, the part that controlled the shear ram was faulty. On the second, the backup battery was dead. There was no automated warning on the rig that would warn the crew that this last line of defense against a catastrophe had lost power.

It's Transocean's responsibility to maintain the rig, including the blowout preventer, in good working order. BP's attorney said at a Coast Guard hearing in Houston that a Transocean maintenance audit done just weeks before the blowout showed the blowout preventer was in disrepair.

The failure of the blowout preventer seemed to shock rig workers and company executives. Tony Hayward repeatedly told congressional investigators that the blowout preventer is "the ultimate failsafe" mechanism for any well. However, studies have shown that blowout preventers are often unreliable. A 2002 MMS study found that only half of the shear rams tested successfully cut a drill pipe in real-world conditions. And only half the companies observed by the researcher chose to test the shear rams when they accepted delivery of new BOP systems.

"If he (Hayward) was stunned, therein lies the problem," said Nansen Saleri. "Critical decisions are being made in this type of misinformed environment." Saleri, who oversaw numerous drilling operations as a senior executive at Saudi Aramco, said in his experience blowout preventers were only 60 to 70 percent reliable. Every person who works on an oil rig should know that failure rate, because that would lead them to be more cautious, Saleri said.

After the crew abandoned ship, the Damon Bankston, a nearby supply vessel, picked up most of the people in the lifeboats and in the water. All nearby boats that heard the mayday call began to fight the inferno on the Horizon.

For hours they poured water on the rig from all sides. Eventually, the weight of the water overwhelmed the ship and it listed, and sank, breaking the riser and drill pipes and unleashing a torrent of crude into the Gulf of Mexico.

● ● ●

"All these things had to happen to get from the initiation to the end of this," Bly said. "At the end of the day, multiple companies, multiple workers and multiple people and decisions, including those by BP, contributed to this."

Assigning blame is crucial to the companies involved, who face massive liabilities from hundreds of civil lawsuits filed not only by the families of workers killed and injured in the disaster, but also from individuals and business owners who say they've lost money or property because of the oil spill, the fishing ban, the drilling moratorium, or the loss of tourism to the Gulf Coast. Criminal penalties could also reach to the billions, since the U.S. government can impose fines for each barrel of oil spilled, each bird injured, and potentially even seek jail time for those responsible. State and local governments may also have claims.

Halliburton and Transocean have criticized Bly's conclusions, accusing BP of trying to divert responsibility to them. "BP's well design and operational decisions compromised well integrity," Halliburton's Vice President for Cementing Thomas Roth said in a National Academy of Sciences hearing.

It may never be certain what exact combination of decisions and functional breakdowns combined to cause the total catastrophe. The investigations showed that workers and managers at BP, Transocean, and Halliburton all made decisions and took actions that might have contributed to the failure of the Macondo well.

In the end, however, one decision stands above the others. BP's and Transocean's rig managers, on the evening of April 20, decided to pump heavy drilling mud out of the Macondo well and replace it with seawater when they weren't certain the well was ready.

Removing the drilling mud is a standard operation before shutting down an exploration well. A Transocean work plan showed the companies intended to begin the displacement around 5:30 P.M. and finish about six hours later.

That morning Donald Vidrine, BP's company man, had an argument with Transocean's offshore installation manager (OIM), Jimmy Harrell, about how to finish the well. Harrell, with thinning white hair, a thick white moustache, and a southern drawl that lends charm to his loose grammar, was supposed to have the ultimate word on everything that happened on the Horizon. As Transocean's top man, he was responsible for the safety of the crew and the safety of the rig. BP had hired Harrell to drill the hole they had designed, but they weren't supposed to be able to tell him how to run the rig. In reality, rig workers say, it doesn't always work that way.

"I recall a scrimmage taking place between the company man, the OIM, and the toolpusher and driller concerning the events of the day," said Doug Brown, the Horizon's chief mechanic. He said the argument was over when and how to displace the mud. "The company man was basically saying, 'Well, this is how it's going to be.' And the toolpusher and the OIM reluctantly agreed."

Harrell minimized the dispute in testimony to Coast Guard investigators, saying he simply told Vidrine he wouldn't begin replacing the drilling mud until they did a negative pressure test, designed to show whether the well is sealed with a barrier strong enough to hold the oil and gas in the undersea reservoir. If the seal doesn't hold, drilling fluid will flow up through the pipe to the rig. "I told him it was my policy to do a negative test before displacing with seawater," said Harrell.

BP had set the cement seal on top of the well unusually deep—about 3,000 feet below the surface—which meant that removing the mud would remove a huge amount of weight from the well. That made the negative pressure test more important than ever.

Harrell was being pressed hard by Vidrine and Robert Kaluza, the second company man, to get the well done and move on to the next job. All three were distracted on that key day because four executives from BP and Transocean were visiting the rig, a visit that was billed as routine, but that revealed tensions between the companies over the slow progress of the well. In one meeting, Harrell told Coast Guard investigators, the group "went over our maintenance plan, trying to get a better—get a good working relationship with the client to where we could meet their needs and they could meet ours."

Harrell spent much of the day meeting with the visitors and missed regular meetings with the crew. At about 3 P.M., rig workers conducted the negative pressure test that Harrell had fought for earlier in the day. During the test, workers remove some drilling mud from the well, reducing the weight on the oil at the bottom. Then they wait to see what happens.

The negative pressure test would be the last test of the well's condition before the Deepwater Horizon would leave Macondo. BP management kept changing plans for that test, confusing the rig crew. As of April 14 the plan was for the crew to put a cement plug in the well, then perform a negative pressure test, then displace the mud from the riser. Those plans changed twice more before April 20. On that morning, according to the President's Oil Spill Commission investigators, the Deepwater Horizon crew were told to pump mud out of the wellbore and perform the negative pressure test before setting a cement plug that might have created an additional barrier against surging gas.

Robert Kaluza, BP's well site manager, speculated in a statement on April 28 about why the plans had changed. "Maybe trying to save time," he said. "At the end of the well, sometimes they think about speeding up."

In the first test, drilling fluid spurted from the pipe, indicating the well wasn't sealed. Wyman Wheeler, a toolpusher, argued with Kaluza about the causes of the bad test. "Wyman was convinced that something wasn't right," said Christopher Pleasant, a subsea engineer who was in the room during the discussion. They were joined by Vidrine and continued to discuss the test for more than an hour. They decided to do a second test, this time using the so-called kill-line, a small pipe connected to the drill pipe.

Those results were bizarre. When they pumped mud from the well pipe, the pressure there rose to 1,400 pounds per square inch, indicating hydrocarbons are trying to force their way up. However, the kill-line pressure didn't change, and no drilling mud came out. Having wildly different pressure in the two connected pipes, BP investigators say, "is not possible." The drillers may have forgotten to open a valve on the kill line, they said.

"I wanted to do another test. I don't know why we didn't see pressure on the kill line," Vidrine told the Coast Guard the night of the explosion. Neither BP nor Transocean had a standard procedure in place on how to conduct or read the results of a negative test. "It's left for the rig to figure out." Transocean's workers said they had seen such results before, and called it a "bladder effect." They apparently convinced BP's managers. Vidrine declined to testify at the Coast Guard Marine Board hearings, citing medical issues. Kaluza also refused to testify, citing his constitutional right against self-incrimination. "The bladder effect doesn't exist," said Sam Clyburn, a lawyer for the Oil Spill Commission. "The question is why these experienced men out on that rig talked themselves into believing this was a good test."

Vidrine called a well engineer at BP's Houston headquarters who told him the well was likely in good shape because he hadn't seen any signs of a kick yet. Since no drilling fluid flowed from the kill line, BP and Transocean managers decided the well must be stable. They were wrong. "During the negative test we didn't see any—anything flow back," Pleasant said. "So, after the negative test, Don told Bob to 'go call the office. Tell them we're going to displace the well.'"

That decision, which removed about 2,600 psi of weight from the well, was the key misstep that led directly to the blowout, experts say.

"Right there is a clear violation of safety standards," says Nansen Saleri, president and CEO of Quantum Reservoir Impact, who worked in reservoir engineering for Saudi Aramco and Chevron. "That was their biggest mistake."

With a volatile well, conflicting or confusing negative test results, and last minute design changes, the managers from BP or Transocean should have stopped the work and sought counsel from their onshore superiors.

"Our OIMs would not have displaced that mud in that riser without going to an operations manager. That would require a VP of the company to sign off on it too," says Phil Tobey, who spent 35 years on offshore rigs, 10 as a rig manager, for Diamond Offshore Drilling, Inc., the largest U.S.-based offshore driller.

BP and Transocean say that anyone on a drilling rig can stop all work if they believe their situation is unsafe. Still, in testimony of dozens of rig workers over weeks of hearings, no one said they or anyone else involved in the decision to remove the heavy mud put their foot down and refused to continue.

"They had multiple red flags," Saleri says. "When you are dealing with this situation, and your own life is in danger, and you're acting as if your life is not in danger, either you're totally incompetent or you are so driven by other imperatives that basically your judgment is flawed." Bartlit said no one on the Deepwater Horizon made a conscious decision to endanger the crew to save money. However, when each day of delay costs more than a million dollars, the pressure hangs over the crew all the time.

The methane likely wouldn't have surged to the surface if the rig managers hadn't pumped the drilling mud from the well. A slow response from the crew or a broken blowout preventer likely wouldn't have mattered.

"Stop, think, don't do something stupid," says Bob Bea.

Chapter 10

BP Struggles to Survive

In late spring, with oil spewing uncontrollably into the Gulf, there were legitimate questions about whether BP would survive at all. Analysts and news reporters openly speculated whether the company would file bankruptcy or become the target of a takeover by a competitor after its stock price plummeted. BP's market value fell by more than half, from about $190 billion before the explosion to $90 billion on June 20, 2010.

Just days after the blast, BP sent remote-controlled vehicles to the sea floor to try to close the valves in the blowout preventer that had earlier failed to stop the blowout. The BOP failed to close a second time. The company tried what seemed like a dozen strategies to stem the flow of crude into the water, efforts with names like "top kill," "top hat," and "junk shot." BP finally resorted to inserting a new pipe into the riser to try to collect some of the oil before it got into the

Gulf. The Coast Guard and Obama's point man on the spill, Admiral Thad Allen, worked closely with BP, but as the oil continued to leak, they began to draw criticism for going too easy on the company that was polluting a precious natural resource. And the city of New Orleans and coastal Louisiana, devastated five years earlier by hurricane Katrina, were likely to take the biggest hit from the oil slick moving across the Gulf.

By April 29, there was already a lot of oil in the Gulf, and it became clear that it could take months to cap the well. The summer tourist and fishing season was in jeopardy. Louisiana officials opened the state's shrimping season early to give fisherman a chance to harvest as much as possible before the oil got to the shore. About two weeks later, Louisiana Governor Bobby Jindal announced that oil had washed ashore in the marshes of Plaquemines Parish. The United States soon closed huge areas of the Gulf to fishing, leaving thousands more residents with no way to make a living, and seafood distributors across the country searching for products and losing money.

Emotions on the Gulf Coast and in Washington were running high. Congressman Charlie Melancon, who represents the marshland regions southwest of New Orleans that are ground zero for the drilling industry and were the first hit by oil, broke down in tears at a May 28 hearing.

"Our culture is threatened, our coastal economy is threatened, and everything I know and love is at risk." He paused, took a breath, and wiped his eyes. "Even though this coast lies . . . along coastal Louisiana, these are America's wetlands." Melancon's voice cracked and his lower lip quivered. He stopped again, unable to control his emotions, and then turned to the committee chair, apologized, and whispered that he'd submit the rest of his statement for the record. He then excused himself and walked out.

● ● ●

BP's reputation was going to take a pounding as long as oil continued to flow into the water. Still, the company could have done more to help itself. Instead of appearing forthright and ready to take responsibility, BP tried initially to deflect blame for the spill to its partners and downplay the size of the spill. Estimates of just how much oil was spewing out of the well kept growing. Immediately after the blowout, BP and U.S. officials said about 1,000 barrels were flowing each day into the Gulf. By late May, the U.S. Geological Survey was saying Macondo was leaking as much at 25,000 barrels a day. The estimates eventually reached a range of 30,000 to 60,000 barrels escaping the well each day.

As the size of the environmental disaster grew, so did the political implications. Washington sprang into action to try to control the damage. President Barack Obama, who only two months earlier had endorsed offshore drilling, announced a six-month ban on new deepwater permits. Attorney General Eric Holder, on June 2, said he was investigating the disaster for both civil and criminal infractions.

The Coast Guard and the Interior Department launched a joint investigation and spent weeks questioning the survivors of the disaster about what exactly happened on the Deepwater Horizon on April 20. The witness' stories allowed the media to recreate the disaster in minute detail while dissecting the clues to speculate on what went wrong and who was at fault.

Congress fed the frenzy. Lawmakers launched a series of investigations, each taking its opportunity to call up BP executives to excoriate them before the television cameras. Waxman and Stupak used their roles on the Energy and Commerce Committee to subpoena hundreds of thousands of pages of documents from BP, Transocean, and Halliburton, and then artfully released them bit by bit as they held weeks of hearings into the causes of the blowout. The anger on Capitol Hill was palpable.

The oil spill had derailed any planned progress on legislation and left the politicians with little to do except show that they were properly angry and ready to do something, once they figured out what. Louisiana Congressman Anh "Joseph" Cao, who five years earlier lost his home to Hurricane Katrina, suggested to BP America President Lamar McKay that suicide might be an option. "In the Asian culture, we do things differently. During the Samurai days, we would just give you a knife and ask you to commit hara-kiri. My constituents are still debating on what they want me to ask you to do."

Industry officials were furious at BP. The drilling moratorium was hurting them all and there was a huge risk that the progress the industry had made on opening new regions to exploration would be reversed. Many remembered when BP's maintenance problems in Alaska closed down the North Slope, costing all the companies that do business there millions. During an Energy Committee hearing, the leaders of all of BP's major rivals took aim at the beleaguered company, saying the company's well design was flawed and that it had taken too many risks. "We would not have drilled the well the way they did," ExxonMobil CEO Rex Tillerson told the committee. Chevron CEO John Watson said, "It certainly appears from your letter that not all standards that we would recommend or that we would employ were in place."

The only way to stop the mounting anger was to stop the oil, which BP proved incapable of doing quickly. Seen from the boardroom of BP, the most dangerous moment came after the failure of "top kill" on May 29. Both BP and the Obama administration had invested heavily in the effort to stop the flow of oil from the Macondo well by pumping heavy drilling mud into it from a ship a mile above on the surface. Tony Hayward and Energy Secretary Steven Chu spent days ensconced at BP's Westlake 4 building, hoping the effort would succeed. When it failed, the administration unleashed its wrath on BP. Obama that day said the failure was "as enraging as it is heartbreaking," and investors began to seriously worry about BP's future. BP's share price plunged, at one point falling 13 percent in one day. By mid-June credit investors were pricing in a 40 percent probability of default.

A week later, Obama announced on national television that he was looking for "some ass to kick."

BP officials pledged over and over again that the company would pay for the entire cleanup and pay all legitimate claims of damage. Still, with speculation emerging that the company might resort to bankruptcy and with no money actually on the table, Congress was suspicious. Democratic lawmakers proposed lifting a legal cap on liabilities so that BP couldn't renege on its pledge even as company executives publicly acknowledged that they would not seek shelter under the $75 million limit. BP and various politicians ended up in an almost farcical argument where members of Congress repeatedly insisted BP must pay for the cleanup, and BP repeatedly assured them it was planning to do so.

BP could have shut down the debate, and the cloud of suspicion, by preemptively throwing money at the problem, says Tony Fratto, a former White House spokesman who helps companies navigate crises in Washington. Fratto says when a high-level BP official sought his counsel in early May, he advised them to set up a fund with an astronomical amount of money in it, and to deposit money into the Treasuries of every Gulf Coast state. "Start writing checks. It will shut up the people who keep saying, 'you're being irresponsible and we'll make you pay.'" BP didn't heed Fratto's advice and instead, as the political rhetoric heated up and lawsuits piled up, wild speculation about BP's eventual liabilities left the market jittery. Interior Secretary Ken Salazar added to the angst on June 9 when he said BP would be required to compensate oil workers laid off because of the government's moratorium on drilling. It looked like the hit to BP might be unlimited.

A fundamental truth in dealing with a crisis that can destroy a company's image is to get all the bad news out fast. In this, BP failed. In addition to creating a fund right away, the company should have immediately given a maximum estimate of the potential oil spill. "If you give everyone a worst case, then all the news after that is good news," Fratto says. "If the reality is worse, then you've got bigger problems than your public image."

BP found no defenders in Washington. Its helplessness in the U.S. capital and ineptness at communications shocked its own board. How could the largest oil and gas producer in the United States, a leader in a regulated industry that's often in the sights of politicians, have so little Washington savvy and so few friends in political and media circles? Part of the problem may have been a tin ear to U.S. politics. Hayward made the rounds with a media advisor, Michele Davis, who had worked in the previous Republican administration for Treasury Secretary Hank Paulson, and the company hired as its top U.S. media representative another Republican aide, Anne Womack Kolton, who had worked in Bush's Energy Department and as a spokesperson for Vice President Dick Cheney. Company executives insisted that they could get just about anyone in Washington on their cell phone, even on weekends. If true, it was doing BP little good.

BP directors worried that the company could be on the road to a financial twilight zone in which it would no longer be able to raise money to fund its operations. The company's financial executives made the rounds of banks asking for commitments of emergency credit lines. The reception must have been sobering. Banks, which in pre-spill days would have considered lending to BP as an almost risk-free deal, now demanded fees reportedly in the tens of millions, to provide backstop loans. The company also raised about $5 billion against future oil receipts from its operations in Angola and Azerbaijan.

There was also a risk that BP's crucial governmental partners around the world would no longer want to do business with Hayward and his crowd. The U.S. Congress was openly discussing barring BP from bidding on new leases in the Gulf. Hayward made the rounds on his jet in July trying to reassure the leaders of Azerbaijan, Russia, and Abu Dhabi, among others and, in the case of the deep-pocketed, pitching them the line that BP stock at its current depressed price was a bargain they should consider.

BP had to stop the bleeding. With warnings from Washington that it would be unconscionable to pay out a dividend in these circumstances, BP executives began looking at the idea of putting the company's $2.6 billion first quarter dividend, which had been declared but would not be paid until June 21, into an escrow account until the spill's victims were compensated. And Dudley sounded out Kenneth Feinberg, the lawyer who had made his reputation administering compensation for the victims of the Sept. 11 attacks to run a Gulf of Mexico fund. BP was initially skeptical of Feinberg, but as it did its due diligence, the company was impressed by his tough, legalistic approach.

The tensions between BP and the administration were high. The company thought it was doing its best to contain the spill and considered the nasty melange of bluster and threats from Washington unhelpful to the main task. After all, BP oil and gas operations had paid billions of dollars in taxes into U.S. coffers in recent years. But the administration was not impressed by what had happened in the past. Obama was being compared with his predecessor, George W. Bush, who was hammered after the federal government botched the response to Hurricane Katrina when it flooded New Orleans, leaving thousands of people homeless, in 2005. Criticism of Obama mounted. Why didn't he stop the well, send in the navy, seize BP's installations?

Robert Reich, a liberal economist and member of President Bill Clinton's cabinet, urged Obama to put BP into federal receivership. "This is the only way the public will know what's going on, be confident enough resources are being put to stopping the gusher, ensure BP's strategy is correct, know the government has enough clout to force BP to use a different one if necessary, and be sure the President is ultimately in charge."

Obama, in truth, had no real option but to rely on BP and the oil industry to eventually come up with a solution. Still, it was an election year for the Congress, and the president's popularity was sinking fast. Republicans threatened to score big in November, and Obama wanted to show that he was not powerless. He couldn't stop the spill, and he couldn't clean it up quickly, but he could extract money from BP. Picking up on a BP idea, he proposed that the company create an escrow fund to pay claims to people and states that had lost money because of the spill. The question that remained was how much. Senate Majority Leader Harry Reid suggested $20 billion in a video posted on his web site on June 14. BP believes the number may have been worked out with the White House.

BP, having heard the criticism about its Republican hires, retained Jamie Gorelick, a former Deputy Attorney General in the Clinton administration, to negotiate the fund with Obama's team. BP was less concerned about the absolute size of the fund than how it would be paid. Though the company earned lots of cash from its oil and gas output, its money wasn't unlimited. If it had to pay $20 billion in one throw, that would risk bankrupting the company, one executive said. The second concern was having a credible administrator who wouldn't succumb to political pressure. The two sides settled on Feinberg, BP's early choice.

On June 16, Chairman Carl-Henric Svanberg, accompanied by Hayward and his soon-to-be successor, Dudley, went to the White House to finalize the agreement that had been scoped-out by Gorelick and White House counsel Robert Bauer. The $20 billion escrow account was close to a done deal. Among the issues that were not resolved was a White House request that BP help oil workers made jobless by the administration's moratorium on drilling. BP took the position that it was not liable for the results of the administration's actions, but in a private Oval Office session, Obama told Svanberg that doing something for these workers was the right thing, and BP agreed to contribute $100 million to a fund, while stressing that this was a voluntary move and not an admission of liability.

Some BP executives were angry and agreed with the characterization by Rep. Joe Barton of Texas of the deal as a "shakedown." As the *Wall Street Journal* said on June 18, "BP's agreement sets a terrible precedent for the economy and the rule of law." BP's board may also have taken legal risks in approving such a large payment without obtaining shareholder approval, although, according to a senior executive, the company received legal advice that it was on safe ground because the payments would be broken up into smaller installments.

Despite the anger at what Obama had done, the company achieved much of what it wanted. The escrow account would be funded not with one lump sum payment but over three and a half years. This long funding period gave the administration an interest in keeping BP in business—something that was not at all clear before. As part of the deal the administration agreed to tone down its rhetoric. Obama acknowledged as much after the meeting with the BP executives, saying: "BP is a strong and viable company and it is in all of our interests that it remain so." BP also credits British Prime Minister David Cameron with helping to persuade Obama to cool down.

BP finally had found a way to establish a relationship with the government. Chief Financial Officer Byron Grote said on a later conference call that for the first time BP had the opportunity "to have a constructive dialogue with the President of the United States and the administration." The collateral for this Gulf of Mexico Oil Spill Trust was the oil and gas production of BP's premier Gulf of Mexico properties: Thunder Horse, Atlantis, Mad Dog, Great White, Mars, Ursa, and Na Kika.

Although the fund did not cap BP's liabilities, and fines will not be paid from the account, the announcement of the deal with the White House calmed the markets. BP no longer seemed headed for a financial meltdown. The "shakedown" may actually have marked the beginning of the turnaround.

● ● ●

Still, the damage to the company and its shareholders was huge. Not only had its stock price plummeted, but BP halted its $10 billion per year dividend, a much more serious blow than the stock fall for pension funds because it deprived them of income that they relied on. Before the Macondo incident, BP provided roughly 14 percent of U.K. corporate dividend payouts in 2009, according to Morgan Stanley, so the company's shares are hugely important to British pension funds and savers. Neil Duncan-Jordan, of the National Pensioners Convention, told the *Daily Telegraph* newspaper: "Most ordinary people would not have thought that BP would have an impact on their retirement, but if BP's share price goes down then their pension pot goes down. Most of those pension funds are invested in the default option, which is stocks and shares, and so if BP goes down the pan then their pension pot goes down the pan."

When it reported results on July 27, BP tried to estimate the extent of the damage, taking a $32.2 billion charge against earnings, leading to an overall loss of $17.2 billion for the second quarter. The charge includes the $20 billion fund. In coming to their estimate, the board assumed that BP would not be found "grossly negligent" in causing the spill. If found grossly negligent, BP could face as much as $17.6 billion in civil penalties, based on a federal panel of experts' estimate on Aug. 2 that about 4.1 million barrels of oil leaked from its well into the Gulf. The Clean Water Act makes BP, as owner of the oil, liable for fines of $1,100 per barrel spilled even if it did nothing wrong, says Wayne State University law professor Noah Hall in Detroit. The penalty jumps to $4,300 per barrel if BP was grossly negligent. Hall says gross negligence in a civil case would include making "conscious decisions" that increased the likelihood of an incident while engaged in a risky business, such as deepwater drilling. A gross negligence finding might also relieve BP's partners, Anadarko Petroleum Corp and a group headed by Japan's Mitsui, of obligations to pay their share of the costs.

Meanwhile, trial lawyers across the South, including Brent Coon, were lining up clients and vying to be part of a steering committee that would coordinate the mounds of litigation. U.S. District Judge

Carl Barbier in New Orleans, in whose courtroom the cases will be tried, estimated there would be thousands of suits filed. BP's partners joined in the attack.

On June 18 Anadarko Petroleum, BP's partner on the Macondo well, put out a statement in the name of its chairman and CEO James Hackett that said in part, "The mounting evidence clearly demonstrates that this tragedy was preventable and the direct result of BP's reckless decisions and actions. Frankly, we are shocked by the publicly available information that has been disclosed in recent investigations and during this week's testimony that, among other things, indicates BP operated unsafely and failed to monitor and react to several critical warning signs during the drilling of the Macondo well. BP's behavior and actions likely represent gross negligence or willful misconduct and thus affect the obligations of the parties under the operating agreement." This repudiation was very damaging for BP. Anadarko, BP's 25 percent partner, and a Mitsui-led group (10 percent) both spurned invoices from BP for its calculations of their share of the costs. But Anadarko may wind up paying huge costs. By early November BP had taken nearly $40 billion in writeoffs for the spill. Having watched Anadarko's behavior, major oil companies may no longer want to team up with smaller ones as partners in Gulf drilling.

The cost to Obama was also growing. While the escrow fund was a political success, the President's other major actions since the blowout have had mixed reviews. His interior department dismantled and recreated the dysfunctional Minerals Management Service and gave it a new name, and the agency has implemented a series of new requirements for offshore operators designed to instill more caution. These measures, however, don't capture the attention of the voting public. His only other concrete action, the drilling moratorium, blew up in his face. Residents of Louisiana, already suffering from the closing of the fishing grounds and loss of tourism, complained that the drilling ban would deprive them of the only source of jobs the region had left.

Obama appeared to be pouring acid on a wide-open wound. At a hearing of the president's commission investigating the causes of the spill, a local fisherman and folk singer brought the crowd to tears when he pulled out his guitar and sang to the stiff-suited bureaucrats about his dying dream of teaching his son to fish in the Mississippi delta. Louisiana Senator Mary Landrieu, a Democrat, blocked Obama's appointee for budget director until the White House lifted the drilling ban.

Two widows of men killed on the Deepwater Horizon publicly advocated for offshore drilling to resume. "While we realize we are suffering from economic impacts resulting from the leaking oil it would be even more devastating if you allow drilling in the gulf to cease," Courtney Kemp, the widow of Roy Wyatt Kemp, told a congressional hearing. "If drilling ceases, not only would offshore employees lose their jobs, but the trickle-down effect would be devastating not only to the coastal states, but eventually to the entire country. You must not allow this to happen. Drilling in the gulf must continue."

● ● ●

To shore up its financial position, BP began putting assets, including Prudhoe Bay in Alaska, on the block. On July 20, BP announced that it would sell Apache Corp. a package of properties in the United States and elsewhere for $7 billion. The properties accounted for about 2 percent of BP's production. The price was more than double BP's in-house valuation. Hayward said on July 27 that the deal effectively valued BP's total exploration and production business at $350 billion—almost 10 times the company's depressed $120 billion market capitalization at the time.

The better-than-expected price encouraged Dudley, the new CEO, to triple the amount of disposals BP might make to $30 billion, cutting production from 3.8 million barrels per day to 3.5 million. What BP has sold and is willing to part with are mostly old onshore or shallow-water fields, where output is declining. The sales will heighten BP's dependence on deepwater fields, which already account for about 18 percent of output. BP's plans for future projects already included a preponderance of deepwater and other challenging areas, such as the Arctic.

Stripped of its plain vanilla fields, BP may come closer to what some of its managers and Wall Street analysts have always wanted it to be and closer to its roots: an aggressive exploration play, dependent on big finds in deep water such as the coastal waters off West Africa and in the Gulf. Under Dudley, the company may also toy with selling off its less profitable refining and marketing wing, as Browne contemplated when he pondered a merger with Shell.

Another result of BP's U.S. problems is likely to be greater dependence on Russia. That shift will be a mixed bag for BP and its shareholders. BP has a unique position there, with a 50 percent stake in Russia's third largest oil company, TNK-BP. But BP's Russian partners are not easy to manage. While Russia is the world's largest oil and gas producer, BP's Russian oil is nowhere near as profitable as some of its U.S. holdings, including the Gulf of Mexico.

With its headaches in the United States, BP can't afford trouble in Russia. Indeed, the Russian affiliate, for now, seems like a godsend, providing cash-pinched BP billions in dividends annually, huge reserves of cheap-to-raise oil, and a safe haven from the blistering criticism it's received in the United States over the handling of its huge spill in the Gulf of Mexico. Russians are "more philosophical" about such mishaps, says Mikhail Fridman, TNK-BP's Chairman.

Both sides now seem to recognize their codependence: The Russians need BP's expertise while BP needs access to Siberia's cheap crude. So BP has backed off, allowing Fridman and his partners to largely run the company their way. The biggest change is a willingness to allow TNK-BP to expand widely abroad. BP was long skeptical of TNK-BP operating beyond the former Soviet Union, which would take the venture into areas where BP has extensive operations of its own. In October BP agreed to sell TNK-BP its businesses in Venezuela and Vietnam for $1.8 billion.

The Russian company's oil fields are money-spinners because of their rock-bottom operating costs. A new field called Ust Vakh was recently developed by the joint venture in West Siberia. And Chief Operating Officer Bill Schrader, a BP veteran, says a frontier area to the East called Yamal could produce up to 900,000 barrels a day in 10 years if adequate pipelines can be built. Given those prospects, Dudley has every reason to keep the bear happy. But, as Hayward found out, that isn't easy.

Dudley won respect for the coolness he displayed under fire in Russia in 2008. He may well have been Browne's choice as a successor. Browne gave Dudley's selection a ringing endorsement, saying: "He is one of the most thoughtful people I know in every sense of the word." Dudley got the nod to lead the entire company, at least in part to placate U.S. politicians and dissuade them from banning BP from drilling in American waters.

Such threats exist. For instance, a drilling overhaul bill passed by the House of Representatives on July 30, 2010, contains a provision written by Rep. George Miller of California, a close ally of Speaker Nancy Pelosi, which would bar any company from drilling in deepwater if more than 10 people had died at its facilities or if it had been fined $10 million or more under the Clean Air or Clean Water Act during a seven year period. BP is the only company that currently meets that description. BP has hit back by saying such measures would make it difficult to pay its obligations in the Gulf.

Nevertheless, Congressman Stupak, who did not run for reelection in 2010, endorsed the plan to punish the company. "Why do we continue to allow these bad actors like BP to access our resources? At what point does the government say we'd like you to bid on our well but you've got such a bad record you're disqualified?" Stupak said in an interview. "BP had Texas City, the North Slope, and now the Deepwater Horizon, and yet they're still saying they want to drill in our environmentally sensitive areas. Why do we allow them? That's insane."

Industry observers think that being forced to sell out of the Gulf or retreat to minority, nonoperating positions would kill morale at the company "If a company with operations the size of BP gives up being an operator in the Gulf of Mexico, then all those technically strong people would start looking for other jobs," says Andrew Gould, CEO of Schlumberger, the largest oil services company.

On July 27, when his new appointment was announced, Dudley made clear that BP planned to remain a leader in the United States and the Gulf of Mexico. "It is not our intention to retreat from the United States, nor do we believe we won't be able to operate there," he said. Over and over again, he has stressed that BP's recovery depends on its meeting its commitments to the United States and cleaning up damage on the Gulf Coast. If so, he posits, BP will be allowed to continue to grow its business in the United States and be "a significant member of the energy community."

"I hope five years from now people will look back and say this was quite an incredible corporate response to a tragic accident," he said, adding that he realized this goal "feels aspirational now."

But Dudley allowed that there could be some U.S. sales, and the company has already begun trimming some of its Gulf portfolio in an effort to reduce future capital expenditure and, possibly, to better position itself for a worst case U.S. reaction. In late September it sold a 20 percent stake in a Gulf of Mexico discovery called Tubular Bells, 135 miles southeast of New Orleans, to its partner Hess Corp. for $40 million. Under the agreement, Hess's interest would rise to 40 percent and it would take over management of the field from BP.

Dudley is not going to have an easy life at the top. What BP now offers investors, governments, and even employees, is a big question mark. The company's own operations have been severely disrupted with vital exploration drilling projects in places such as Libya delayed and the inability to drill in the Gulf of Mexico cutting production at Thunder Horse. In an interview in June 2010 in Washington, just after the establishment of the escrow fund, Dudley acknowledged that the Gulf oil spill had been a severe blow to employee morale. Thanks to Browne's Beyond Petroleum campaign, BP employees had a certain esprit de corps based on seeing themselves as "part of the long-term transition to a lower hydrocarbon" economy, he said. It will take a long time to recover that good feeling.

Dudley's most difficult task is showing that he can bring a fresh perspective to BP. There is a conviction in the oil industry that bringing in outsiders to run major oil companies will only lead to trouble, but BP is a company that would seem to be crying out for fresh blood. The pool from which chief executives at BP are selected seems strikingly small and insular, particularly considering the company's global reach. He also needs to be sure that his safety drive doesn't snuff out BP's creative flair, the strength of the company.

Dudley also suggested that there could be a silver lining to the Macondo disaster, with BP becoming a company with "higher quality assets and growth." It's not total fantasy. The size of BP and the other majors makes it difficult for them to replace the oil they produce, let alone grow because they need to discover enormous quantities of oil each year just to keep pace with what they pump from the ground. They are also trading at substantial discounts to the sum of their parts. Small exploration and production companies receive higher multiples from the financial markets. BP and the other majors are also tied to paying substantial dividends, which cuts into their ability to make further investments.

Still, Fadel Gheit, the Oppenheimer & Co. analyst, doubted that BP would benefit from the spill. BP "will never be as good as before," he said. "This is like a guy suffering a massive stroke. No company that pays liabilities of $30 to $60 billion is better for it. Their opportunities are reduced. You are making BP work for two to three years for no profit. [They] are giving all the profit away to the fishermen, the cleaners, and the government." Gheit said that while BP would become smaller it would survive.

On the other hand, during its century in business, BP has shown a knack for coming back from setbacks. And it retains tremendous earnings power. The company would have made about $8 billion in the second quarter if there had been no spill. BP has already been able to return to the markets to sell $3.5 billion in bonds in late September. The offer was about four times oversubscribed. "People were amazed at the ease with which BP was able to generate enormous sums of money selling nonstrategic assets," said J. Robinson West, Chairman of Washington-based PFC Energy. "The financial scale of these companies is amazing."

• • •

The legacy of the Macondo blowout may be a revamp of the macho world of offshore drilling. The investigations have painted a portrait of an industry with poorly developed operating standards and inadequate regulation. On November 9, 2010, William K. Reilly, co-chair of the National Commission on the BP Deepwater Horizon Oil Spill, criticized what he called "a culture of complacency." Reilly pointed out that that the three companies "implicated in this disaster," BP, Halliburton, and Transocean, "are major, respected companies operating throughout the Gulf," yet "the evidence is they are in need of top-to-bottom reform."

One of Dudley's first acts as CEO was to abolish the headstrong exploration and production division, leaving no place for Inglis, who was replaced by three people with smaller portfolios. Insiders say the aim is to centralize decision-making in the hands of the CEO and make BP more like ExxonMobil. Dudley appeared to acknowledge that the Deepwater Horizon incident had revealed flaws in BP's culture and structure. "There are lessons for us relating to the way we operate, the way we organize our company, and the way we manage risk," he said. He also announced the establishment of a safety and risk management group reporting directly to the CEO. A person responsible for safety will be planted in each key unit and, in theory, will be able to veto decisions that make him or her uncomfortable "These are the first and most urgent steps I am putting in place to rebuild trust in BP," he said. BP employees, he said, should not be put in a position where they had to make a choice between "commercial economics" and safety. To underline his point, he made the bonuses for the fourth quarter of 2010, the first quarter in which he was fully in control, entirely based on safety, compliance, risk management, and "exhibiting and reinforcing the right behaviors consistent with these goals."

●●●

The Interior Department, meantime, issued a series of new safety rules designed to force companies to place disaster prevention on par with profit. Companies will have to set up a safety management structure that would focus on overall system safety, similar to what Dudley created at BP. Salazar is also requiring companies to have their safety practices independently analyzed, and their blowout preventers certified by a third party.

The rest of the industry was doing what it could to stay in business in the Gulf of Mexico. Led by ExxonMobil, a group of the largest companies including Chevron, Shell, and ConocoPhillips announced they were designing and building a standby containment system for deepwater blowouts that would allow them to cap blown-out wells and capture most of the oil before it spreads through the Gulf. Operated by a nonprofit company, the Marine Well Containment Company, the new system would receive an initial investment of $1 billion, and it would be designed to do all the things that BP and the industry so miserably failed to do after the Macondo blowout. The apparatus would look much like what BP used to eventually capture a portion of the oil and channel it to the surface.

The disaster has offered a window into the world of offshore oil exploration and drilling to a voting public who, only two years earlier had chanted "drill, baby, drill" while knowing little about what that actually meant. Voters by the fall of 2010 had learned that there were already thousands of offshore wells and platforms in the Gulf, and that many had been there for decades. They also saw the devotion to the industry of the residents of the Gulf Coast, those who had been most hurt by the spill. This was a home-grown, high-tech industry that still offered high-paying jobs to people with little education or other prospects.

Given that oil from deepwater installations is needed to assure future supplies, it seems unlikely that the march into deeper water will be halted. Projections prior to the spill showed deepwater production doubling over the next five years to 10 million barrels per day. Roughly half of all discoveries between 2006 and 2009 came from deepwater drilling. Given that success, it is unlikely that offshore drilling will slow significantly outside the United States.

Even in the United States, the demand for energy means deepwater drilling will continue. Obama lifted the moratorium on deepwater drilling on October 12, 2010, less than six months after the Deepwater Horizon exploded. The Gulf of Mexico accounted for about 30 percent of U.S. oil output or about 1.6 million barrels per day in 2009, a 400,000 barrel increase over 2008. Most of this increase came from deepwater fields including Thunder Horse and Atlantis.

But drilling will likely become more expensive. Christophe de Margerie, CEO of Total, estimates delays and costs in the Gulf of Mexico will rise by 20 percent. But most countries around the world have examined their drilling regimes and found them basically sound. Saudi Arabia has said it will go ahead with a new program of deepwater exploration in the Red Sea. As long as consumers need oil and gas, there is little choice but to go into deep water to find new supplies. The governments of oil producing countries, which depend on the international oil industry for revenues, may warn and threaten, but they are unlikely to shoo the golden geese away.

Epilogue

A panicky call came: "John Browne is here. Will you come over and entertain him?"

Business Week had been trying to persuade John Browne to speak at its fall editorial conference in London for years. In 2007, he finally agreed. Then came his resignation. The organizers fretted about whether he would come at all. He honored the commitment; he even came early. Hence, the panic. When a journalist he knew arrived to keep him company, Browne was initially wary. "I never need to speak to people like you again," he said. But then, sitting on a bench in a corridor at Claridge's Hotel, he proceeded to talk cordially and at length. Leaving BP may have been something he dreaded when he was there, but doing so had proved a huge relief. He had given up his cigar habit the day he left, he said. He felt much better.

Later, he gave a talk on the business opportunities offered by the current moment of seismic change in the energy industry that the audience agreed was a tour de force. It is not possible to predict what forms of energy will emerge as dominant, he said, but he suggested that business could succeed by adopting certain principles, among them flexibility, a collaborative approach, and a drive to use energy efficiently. Browne believes, given the sheer scale of the increase in future energy demand, all energy sources—high carbon and low carbon—will grow side-by-side, for a long period of time. His message is both urgent and hopeful: "We have a crucial period of around 50 years in which we must change, must invent and must learn to tap a much broader array of energy sources. It is an existential challenge. However, we have the time to carry out the transition in an orderly manner."

Browne's day job is now Managing Partner for Europe of the private equity fund Riverstone LLC. His presence at the fund has helped attract about $10 billion from pension funds and other sources of capital for both renewable energy and conventional energy investments. During his former company's ordeal he has kept out of the spotlight, relieved that he is no longer in charge. His reputation is recovering from the battering it took on his departure from BP. The new British government of Prime Minister David Cameron has made him a high profile adviser on the financing of universities, and in October 2010, he recommended the lifting of the current roughly $5,000 ceiling on tuition fees. And he is still sought as a guru on how to deal with climate change. Browne has mostly escaped association with the Macondo incident, although he has occasionally encountered criticism. At a book festival in Edinburgh, Scotland in August 2010, he rejected suggestions that measures he presided over could have led to the Gulf of Mexico disaster. But he admitted that trust in BP had been badly damaged and said that BP's move toward more sustainable energy sources had "stalled."

Lawyers will likely spend years trying to establish who was to blame for the Gulf of Mexico spill. But the cause may never be crystal clear. And the effort may not be of the greatest importance. Across the world, people use about 85 million barrels of oil each day.

Americans use about 20 million. We have used up the easy-to-reach sources of these fuels. As a consequence the industry is moving into more and more treacherous environments. It is in all of our interests to make sure that the industry adopts the safest possible practices, but we should not delude ourselves into thinking that risk can ever be completely eliminated. Ultimately, all of us who consume oil and gas in large quantities are responsible for what the oil industry does to find and produce these substances.

The oil industry is inherently dangerous but, for now, necessary. Even the people most hurt by the Deepwater Horizon tragedy understand this. Natalie Roshto, a young mother whose 22-year-old husband Shane was killed on April 20, has spent the ensuing months campaigning to make offshore exploration safer rather than calling for its elimination. She told a congressional committee:

> I fully support offshore drilling because, like Shane, many men and women depend on this as a means to provide for their families and to provide our country with a commodity that is a necessary part of everyday life. I would like to leave here today knowing that because of the tragic death of my husband, we can begin to focus on making safety the *most* important priority.

It is hard not to have respect for those who seek new sources of energy far at sea and deep in the earth. In an essay on an exhibition of books and objects on early navigation at Washington's Folger Shakespeare Library, Edward Rothstein of the *New York Times* compares today's oil explorers to the seafarers of past centuries and the dangers they faced:

> The oil spill might seem a completely man-made mess, the result of some careless drilling, but the nature of the enterprise—plumbing the ocean's resources, daring the dangers of the deep, risking lives to fill elemental needs—is unthinkable

without taking the sea's powers and promise into account. Perhaps off-shore drilling is a contemporary form of nineteenth-century whaling, even in the object of the quest.

The nineteenth-century mariners hunted whales for their oil, the illuminant of the day. It is not preposterous to say that BP and the other oil companies have replaced them in a risky and elemental quest. The oil workers across the Gulf coast, such as Mike Williams, Doug Brown, Stephen Bertone and their colleagues in the oil towns on the edge of the North Sea, on the coasts of Africa, Brazil and Australia, are carrying on that legacy. Some of them, like Shane Roshto, have paid the ultimate price.

Acknowledgments

There are only two names on the front of this book, but it was a much larger group that helped us make it come together. We'd like to take all the credit, but nobody would believe us.

So here goes:

We interviewed dozens of people who gave generously of their time, knowledge, and sometimes even hospitality (i.e., coffee) to ensure that the words on these pages were well-informed. Some are quoted here and others are not, but every one of them helped us to better understand the oil industry, offshore drilling, safety, and regulation, and for that we are grateful.

We also thank Bloomberg News, and our editor-in-chief, Matt Winkler, for asking us to write this book and giving us whatever resources we needed. Because of Bloomberg's commitment to this story and this project, we were able to meet our sources in person, attend hearings, speak to victims, and get a firsthand look at BP's Russian joint venture. The number of news organizations with the resources and willingness to spend time and money on a great story is shrinking, and we're glad we're working for one of them.

Laurie Hays helped with the early conceptualization, read drafts, and was an enthusiastic supporter throughout. Reto Gregori gave us carte blanche backing. Susan Warren made incisive comments and provided virtual tea and sympathy. Amanda Bennett, Al Hunt, Mike Tackett, and Bob Blau set us free to write.

Our Bloomberg colleagues gave generously to this book—whether they were aware of it or not.

Joe Carroll spent many months in 2010 in Louisiana and Houston—far from his home—helping inform the world about what happened on the Deepwater Horizon. We borrowed freely—stole?—from his reporting, and we thank him for all his hard work.

In addition to Joe, many other colleagues' work and support made this book possible. They include Tim Coulter, Will Kennedy, Edward Klump, Amanda Jordan, Jessica Resnick-Ault, Jim Polson, Brett Foley, Katarzyna Klimasinska, Jim Efstathiou, Brian Swint, Laurel Calkins, Rose Brady, Chris Power, Jim Ellis, David Wethe, Ellen Joan Pollock, David Rocks, Larry Liebert, Eduard Gismatullin, Julianna Goldman, Kim Chipman, Ryan Chilcote, Lizzie O'Leary, Julie Slattery, Jim Snyder, Torrey Clark, Stephen Bierman, Kari Lundgren, Peter Coy, Josh Tyrangiel, Lisa Lerer, Robin Ajello, Jeff Taylor, Joe Winski, Brian Bremner, Cristina Lindblad, Paul Barrett, and Steve Adler. We're lucky to have been surrounded by such a great team.

Seth Myers in Bloomberg's graphics department created art for this book, patiently enduring our less-than-specific instructions and divining what we needed. Plus, he got married in the middle of it all. Congratulations!

We would also like to thank Anita Kumar, Michael Novatkoski, and the rest of the staff at the Bloomberg Library, who responded to our many research requests.

We would also like to thank the many people who have helped us over the years to better understand the oil industry. They include

Acknowledgments

John Browne, Tony Hayward, Robert Dudley, Andy Inglis, David Rainey, Cindy Yeilding, Jeroen van der Veer, Andrew Gould, J. Robinson West, Daniel Yergin, Greg Coleman, Fergus MacLeod, Jim Farnsworth, Michael Daly, Edward Morse, Peter Jackson, Mikhail Fridman, Maurice Dijols, Bill Schrader, Ibrahim al Muhanna, Peter Charow, Raad Alkadiri, Roger Diwan, Roddy Kennedy, Andrew Gowers, Toby Odone, Robert Wine, Michele Davis, David Nicholas, Alec Mikhailiants, Daren Beaudo, Scott Dean, Stuart Bruseth, Charles Richards, and Stephen Whittaker.

Many others generously offered their time and insights to shed light on the Deepwater Horizon tragedy, including Don Fitzgerald, Karlene Roberts, Nansen Saleri, Nancy Leveson, Amy Myers Jaffe, Kenneth B. Medlock III, Martin Lovegrove, Don van Nieuwenhuise, Glenn Murray, Larry Dickerson, Tom Lowenstein, Ben Bagert, Jimmy Delery, Tony Fratto, Brent Coon, Matthew Shaffer, Dennis McElwee, David Senko, Jay Jackson, Matt Resell, Greg McCormack, Bart Stupak, Norm Szydlowski, Scott Schloegel, Jason Grumet, Bill Reilly, Paul Bledsoe, Pete Nelson, Eileen Claussen, and others who'd rather not see their names here. Robert Bea welcomed us into his home for many hours, and even offered lunch.

The creative and talented Tymalyn James won the title contest when she e-mailed in with the three words "In Too Deep." Thanks for letting us use it. We owe you a lollipop.

If we left your name off this list, please forgive us. We still think you're fabulous.

Our editors at John Wiley & Sons, Pamela van Giessen and Emilie Herman, were steady and calm as they guided us through this project. Simone Black cheered us with her e-mails. And Steve Isaacs at Bloomberg helped kick the project off.

Stanley wants to thank Norman Pearlstine, Tim Quinson, and David Ellis for helping him with the transition to Bloomberg.

Alison would like to thank the ladies at Capital City Cheesecake in Takoma Park, Maryland, who kept her fully caffeinated and provided her with a tabletop, an outlet, and the occasional luscious little key lime cheesecake. This book is certainly better because of their contribution.

Special thanks to Jennifer Fitzgerald for turning over her apartment and sweet dog Boone in the homestretch so her sister would have a quiet place to work. Nikita, Elijah, and Forrest dealt with the absence of their mom with their usual good humor.

Above all we'd like to thank our spouses—Drew Kodjak and Katherine Reed—who released us from our familial obligations and encouraged us both to dive headlong into this project. They each read early drafts of the book and helped us to make it better. You are both wonderful.

Notes

Prologue

Page 2 "The *New Yorker* magazine . . ." Patricia Marx, "The BP 'I Hate to Clean Up' Cookbook," *New Yorker*, June 28, 2010.

Page 3 "As Amy Myers Jaffe . . ." Stanley Reed, Jessica Resnick-Ault, and Brian Swint, "BP Faces Extra Obstacles After Spill," *Bloomberg Business Week*, May 31–June 6, 2010.

Chapter 1: Night of Horror, Day of Triumph

Page 5 "Through the phone . . ." Testimony of Michael Williams at the Coast Guard Marine Board of Investigation Hearing in Kennar, Louisiana, July 23, 2010.

Page 6 "Doug Brown, the chief mechanic . . ." Testimony of Doug Brown at the Coast Guard Marine Board of Investigation Hearing in Kennar, Louisiana, May 26, 2010.

Page 7 "It was higher . . ." Testimony of Michael Williams at the Coast Guard Marine Board of Investigation Hearing in Kennar, Louisiana, July 23, 2010.

Page 7 "I was wondering . . ." Testimony of Doug Brown at the Coast Guard Marine Board of Investigation Hearing in Kennar, Louisiana, May 26, 2010.

Page 7 "After the first explosion . . ." Transcript of Stephen Bertone testimony to the Coast Guard Marine Board of Investigation in Kennar, Louisiana, July 19, 2010.

Page 7 "Williams was crawling . . ." Testimony of Michael Williams at the Coast Guard Marine Board of Investigation Hearing in Kennar, Louisiana, July 23, 2010.

Page 7 "Brown, who had pulled . . ." Douglas A. Blackmon, Vanessa O'Connell, Alexandra Berson, and Ana Campoy, "There Was Nobody in Charge," *Wall Street Journal*, May 27, 2010; and testimony of Stephen Bertone to the Coast Guard Marine Board of Investigation in Kennar, Louisiana, July 19, 2010.

Page 8 "Brown helped Williams . . ." Ibid.

Page 9 "I honestly didn't . . ." Testimony of Michael Williams at the Coast Guard Marine Board of Investigation Hearing in Kennar, Louisiana, July 23, 2010.

Page 12 "We don't do simple . . ." Stanley Reed, "BP Keeps Rolling the Dice," *BusinessWeek,* September 14, 2009.

Page 16 "Within an hour . . ." Paul Purpura, "Terror, Daring Rescue in Gulf of Mexico Oil Rig Explosion Recounted," *Times-Picayune*, May 7, 2010.

Chapter 2: The Oil Lord

Page 21 "Here's to Russia, . . ." Stanley Reed, "The Oil Lord," *BusinessWeek*, Oct. 27, 2003.

Page 24 "His technological flair . . ." John Browne, *Beyond Business: An Inspirational Memoir from a Visionary Leader* (London: Weidenfeld & Nicolson, 2010), 33.

Page 24 "Not your typical oilman . . ." Ginny Dougary, "Lord Browne, 'I'm Much Happier Now than I've Ever Been,'" *The Sunday Times*, February 6, 2010.

Page 25 "At Stanford in the 1980s . . ." John Browne, *Beyond Business*, 46.

Page 25 "But I little realized then . . ." Ibid., 45.

Page 25 "So her presence, he said . . ." Ibid., 216.

Page 25 "In 1982 he devised . . ." Ibid., 47.

Page 26 "BP quickly stopped . . ." Ibid., 49.

Page 26 "If everything is cut . . ." Stanley Reed, "The Oil Lord," *BusinessWeek*, October 27, 2003.

Page 27 "He even gave a . . ." Browne, *Beyond Business*, 68.

Page 27 "He also believed . . ." Ibid., 69.

Page 27 "When a last meeting . . ." Ibid., 70.

Page 28 "It seems to me . . ." Ibid., 58.

Page 30 "As the negotiations . . ." Ibid., 71.

Page 30 "It was Browne's . . ." Dudley White, "Amoco: The Jewel in Browne's Collectors Crown," Bloomberg News, August 11, 1998.

Page 32 "He decided that if . . ." Browne, *Beyond Business*, 81.

Page 32 "In May, 1997 . . ." Browne, *Beyond Business*, 77.

Page 32 "The time to consider . . ." Text of John Browne's speech, "Addressing Global Climate Change" (May 19, 1997). Retrieved from www .bp.com/genericarticle.do?categoryId=98&contentId=2000427.

Page 32 "One was Fred Krupp . . ." Browne, *Beyond Business*, 85.

Page 33 "Beyond Petroleum" itself . . ." Ibid., 194.

Page 34 "*Mother Jones* magazine pointed out . . ." Bill McKibbon, "Hype vs. Hope," *Mother Jones*, November/December 2006.

Page 35 "Now was the time . . ." Browne, *Beyond Business*, 59–60.

Page 36 "And Browne admits . . ." Ibid., 196.

Page 37 "It was 2005 when Browne . . ." Ibid., 128.

Page 38 "Browne was summoned . . ." Ibid., 115–116.

Page 39 "BP insiders say . . ." Stanley Reed, "The Oil Lord," *BusinessWeek*, October 27, 2003.

Page 43 "On his 2003 visit . . ." Ibid.

Chapter 3: Agents of Empire

Page 47 "In what would become . . ." Daniel Yergin, *The Prize* (New York: Simon & Schuster, 1991), 135.

Page 47 "He took 10,000 pounds . . ." Berry Ritchie, *Portrait in Oil: An Illustrated History of BP* (London: James & James, 1995), 10.

Page 47 "This is how . . ." Ibid., 12.

Page 48 "Every purse has its limits, . . ." Yergin, *The Prize*, 139.

Page 48 "That discovery and subsequent finds . . ." Ritchie, *Portrait in Oil*.

Page 49 "Reynolds, who repeatedly clashed . . ." Yergin, *The Prize*, 147.

Page 50   "They controlled 63 percent . . ."   James Bamberg, *British Petroleum and Global Oil 1950–1975: The Challenge of Nationalism* (Cambridge, UK: Cambridge University Press, 2000), 205.

Page 50   "By the early twenty-first century . . ."   Stanley Reed, "Why You Should Worry About Big Oil," *BusinessWeek*, May 15, 2006.

Page 51   "Between 1945 and 1950 . . ."   Yergin, *The Prize*, 451.

Page 51   "An Iranian observer described . . ."   Stephen Kinzer, *All the Shah's Men: An American Coup and the Roots of Middle East Terror* (Hoboken, NJ: John Wiley & Sons, 2003), 67.

Page 52   "Anglo-Iranian's Chairman . . ."   Ibid., 68.

Page 52   "*Time* made him . . ."   Ibid., 133.

Page 52   "In a speech . . ."   Ibid., 123.

Page 53   "You do not know . . ."   Ibid., 105.

Page 53   "Never had so few . . ."   Ibid., 206.

Page 54   "Eisenhower was eventually convinced . . ."   Ibid., 163.

Page 54   "Still, discoveries in Libya . . ."   Ritchie, *Portrait in Oil*, 83.

Page 54   "By 1976 its equity . . ."   Ritchie, *Portrait in Oil*, 92.

Page 55   "In 1970, the Sea Quest . . ."   Bamberg, *British Petroleum and Global Oil 1950–1975: The Challenge of Nationalism*, 201–203.

Page 55   "Production platforms for the Forties . . ."   Ritchie, *Portrait in Oil*, 98.

Page 56   "Tired of drilling dry holes . . ."   Bamberg, *British Petroleum and Global Oil, 1950–1975: The Challenge of Nationalism*, 192–195.

Page 56   "Though their reserves . . ."   Yergin, *The Prize*, 574.

Page 56   "Those big discoveries . . ."   Bamberg, *British Petroleum and Global Oil, 1950–1975: The Challenge of Nationalism*, 206.

Page 57   "BP encountered obstacles . . ."   Yergin, *The Prize*, 665.

Page 57   "Without the Trans Alaska pipeline . . ."   Browne, *Beyond Business*, 40.

Chapter 4: The Big Kahuna of the Gulf

Page 61   "Oil fields with more than 500 million . . ."   World Resources Institute, "Size Distribution of Oil Fields." Retrieved from http://archive.wri.org/newsroom/wrifeatures_text.cfm?ContentID=381.

Page 65   "Adding to their angst . . ."   C.A. Yeilding, *The History of a New Play: The Thunderhorse Discovery Deepwater Gulf of Mexico* (The American Association of Petroleum Geologists, 2005).

Page 65 "Every explorer is physically . . ." Ibid.

Page 68 "Then in 2006 defective welds . . ." "Deepwater Horsepower," BP website.

Page 68 "When BP is good . . ." *Horizon*, November 2007, 10.

Page 68 "It earns the company . . ." Stanley Reed, Brian Swint, and Jessica Resnick-Ault, "BP Faces Extra Obstacles After Spill," *Bloomberg BusinessWeek*, May 31–June 6, 2010, 19.

Page 70 "It's already the world's . . ." Stanley Reed, "Why Robert Dudley's BP Could Be Even Riskier," *Bloomberg BusinessWeek*, July 28, 2010.

Page 70 "There is an enormous amount . . ." Stanley Reed, Joe Carroll, Rachel Layne, and Jessica Resnick-Ault, "The Paradox of Deepwater: Lots of Oil, Lots of Danger," *Bloomberg BusinessWeek*, May 17–23, 2010, 17.

Page 70 "These are highly compensated people . . ." Stanley Reed, Brian Swint, David Wethe, and Torrey Clark, "Why the U.S. Can't Turn Its Back on BP," *Bloomberg BusinessWeek*, June 28–July 4, 2010, 13–14.

Page 74 "Inglis at the time said . . ." BP Press release, September 2, 2009.

Page 74 "This is something that . . ." Edward Klump and Stanley Reed, "How BP's Spill Tarred Anadarko Petroleum," *Bloomberg BusinessWeek*, July 22, 2010.

Page 77 "For the eight years . . ." Stanley Reed, "BP Keeps Rolling the Dice," *BusinessWeek*, September 14, 2009, 48.

Chapter 5: Money, Politics, and Bad Timing

Page 79 "This tiny town of Cajuns . . ." "The Economic Impacts of Port Fourchon on the National and Houma MSA Economics," Loren Scott & Associates, April 2008, retrieved from www.portfourchon.com/site100-01/1001757/docs/port_fourchon_economic_impact_study.pdf.

Page 79 "Those oil platforms produce 30 percent . . ." "The Economic Impact of the Gulf of Mexico Offshore Oil and Natural Gas Industry and the Role of the Independents," *IHS Global Insight*, July 21, 2010.

Page 82 "BP acknowledged in 2005 . . ." Jim Efstahiou Jr., "BP's U.S. Unit Says Officials Met with Cheney Energy Task Force," Bloomberg News, November 30, 2005.

Page 82 "Two months later . . ." Documents from the Natural Resources Defense Council website, obtained by FOIA.

Page 84 "Oil and gas companies spent . . ." from Center for Responsive Politics, Opensecrets.com.

Page 84 "In July 2005, the House and Senate . . ." Jonathan Salant, "U.S. Energy Industry's Lobbying Pays Off with Aid," Bloomberg News, July 27, 2005.

Page 89 "Alaska, which doesn't charge . . ." Alison Fitzgerald, "Palin Boosted Oil-Company Taxes While Alaska Had Budget Surplus," Bloomberg News, September 6, 2008.

Page 91 "A report in 2010 showed . . ." Jim Polson, "MMS Employees Took Gifts, Viewed Porn, Report Funds," Bloomberg News, May 25, 2010.

Page 92 "Frank Patton, the MMS drilling engineer . . ." Transcript of testimony by Frank Patton to the U.S. Marine Board of Investigation, May 11, 2010.

Page 93 "Given what happened after the Macondo blowout . . ." Alison Fitzgerald, "BP Prepared for Spill 10 Times Gulf Disaster, Permit Plan Says," Bloomberg News, May 31, 2010.

Page 93 "Hayward acknowledged the company . . ." Ed Crooks, "BP 'Not Prepared' for Spill," *Financial Times*, June 3, 2010.

Chapter 6: Lord Browne's Long Goodbye

Page 99 "The company had grown . . ." "Group Strategy: Presentation to the BP PLC Board of Directors," BP presentation, September 2003.

Page 100 "In late July 2006 . . ." Carola Hoyos, "Row Over BP Chief's Succession," *Financial Times*, July 24, 2006.

Page 100 "For instance, a July 24 article . . ." Ibid.

Page 100 "Merrill Lynch, for instance . . ." Ibid.

Page 100 "A truly civilized society . . ." Browne, *Beyond Business*, 212.

Page 101 "In his book Browne admits . . ." Ibid., 213.

Page 103 "Brown said the company . . ." from Bloomberg News video recording of Browne's press conferences.

Page 105 "BP's own internal report . . ." Management Accountability Project, "Texas City Isomerization Explosion," Final Report, February 2007.

Page 106 "Within weeks of the blast . . ." Mimi Swartz, "Eva vs. Goliath," *Texas Monthly*, July 2007.

Page 108 "A 1999 business plan said . . ." Texas City Business Unit Business Strategy, October 1999.

Page 108 "a BP internal report concluded that . . ." "Investigation Report: Refinery Explosion and Fire (15 killed, 180 injured)," U.S. Chemical Safety and Hazard Investigation Board, March 2007.

Page 109 "The share price averaged . . ." from Bloomberg data.

Page 110 "The year before the explosion . . ." "Investigation Report: Refinery Explosion and Fire (15 killed, 180 injured)," U.S. Chemical Safety and Hazard Investigation Board, March 2007.

Page 110 "BP was the only oil company . . ." Lise Olsen, "BP Refinery Deaths Top Industry in U.S.," *Houston Chronicle*, May 16, 2005.

Page 111 "An investigation by the Chemical Safety Board . . ." "Investigation Report: Refinery Explosion and Fire, BP, Texas City, Texas," U.S. Chemical Safety and Hazard Investigation Board, March 23, 2005 (released March 2007), retrieved from www.csb.gov/assets/document/CSBFinalReportBP .pdf.

Page 112 "BP commissioned a separate panel . . ." Report of the BP U.S. Refineries Independent Safety Review Panel, July 16, 2007.

Page 113 "The report concluded that at Texas City . . ." Management Accountability Project, "Texas City Isomerization Explosion," February 2007, retrieved from www.contractormisconduct.org/ass/contractors/61/ cases/808/938/bp-amoco-2005-refinery-explosion_report.pdf.

Page 113 "In 2006 BP's board cut . . ." Stephen Voss, "BP Cuts Browne's Annual Bonus Over Safety Issues," Bloomberg News, March 6, 2007.

Page 113 "Frequency: The big bad wolf blows . . ." BP internal presentation entitled "BP Group HSE Standard, Major Accident Risk Awareness Training," Oct. 17, 2002.

Page 114 "According to the *Wall Street Journal* . . ." Chip Cummins, Carrick Mollenkamp, Aaron O. Patrick, and Guy Chazan, "Scandal, Crises Hasten Exit for British Icon—BP Chief's Tenure Was Increasingly Rocky; Then He Lied to Court—Hiding an Escort Service," *Wall Street Journal*, May 2, 2007.

Page 115 "Nearly 10 years into his tenure . . ." Browne, *Beyond Business*, 200-1.

Page 116 "At the end of 2008 . . ." Carola Hoyos, "Sutherland Wins BP Power Play," *Financial Times*, July 26, 2006.

Page 116 "Browne told reporters that he and Sutherland . . ." Chip Cummins and Carrick Mollenkamp, "Deals & Deal Makers: BP Chairman Tries to Guide Firm Beyond Missteps—Sutherland's Profile Rises Amid Probes, Leadership Transition," *Wall Street Journal*, February 8, 2007.

Page 116 "He was with friends in Barbados . . ."   Browne, *Beyond Business*, 219.

Page 116 "Browne reacted by retaining a law firm . . ."   Ibid., 215–216.

Page 116 "By the time Browne met Chevalier . . ."   Dennis Rice, "The True Story About Lord Browne—by Ex-Rent Boy Lover," *Mail Online*, May 6, 2007.

Page 116 "According to an article . . ."   Ibid.

Page 117 "The perks were stupendous . . ."   Ibid.

Page 117 "carefully crafted e-mail" . . ."   Browne, *Beyond Business*, 215.

Page 117 "facing hunger and homelessness" . . ."   "BP Chief and Ex-Boyfriend: Full Text of Judgment," *The Times*, May 1, 2007.

Page 117 "He condemned Browne's untruth . . ."   Ibid.

Page 118 "It was intrusive and unpleasant, . . ."   Browne, *Beyond Business*, 221.

Page 118 "Browne now admits . . ."   Ibid., 223.

Page 118 "For far too long BP's board . . ."   Jeffrey Sonnenfeld, "Governance by Cliché or Judgment?" *BusinessWeek*, May 17, 2007.

Chapter 7: Riding the Throughput Curve

Page 119 "BP began developing its first field . . ."   BP in Alaska, BP, July 2009. Retrieved from www.bp.com/liveassets/bp_internet/globalbp/STAGING/global_assets/downloads/A/abp_wwd_alaska_bp_in_alaska_2009.pdf.

Page 120 "Browne ordered his workers . . ."   Browne, *Beyond Business*, 209.

Page 122 "The decision "will shorten . . ."   BP internal emails, *Congressional Record*, May 16, 2007.

Page 122 "One contractor complained to BP . . ."   Ibid.

Page 129 "*BusinessWeek* ran an article . . ."   Steve Levine, "Exxon: Juggernaut or Dinosaur?" *BusinessWeek*, February 5, 2009.

Page 131 "The company's own report said . . ."   "Investigation Report: Refinery Explosion and Fire (15 killed, 180 injured)," U.S. Chemical Safety and Hazard Investigation Board, March 2007, 145.

Page 133 "We need to ensure that . . ."   BP Texas City Site Report of Findings, "Texas City's Protection, Performance, Behaviors, Culture, Management and Leadership," The Telos Group, January 21, 2005.

Page 134 "The company accounted for . . ."   Jim Morris and M.B. Pell, "Renegade Refiner: OSHA Says BP Has Systemic Safety Problem," May 16, 2010, retrieved from www.publicintegrity.org/articles/entry/2085/.

Chapter 8: Tony Hayward Comes Up Short

Page 139 "John has been . . ." BP internal communication, May 3, 2007.

Page 140 "We weren't listening . . ." "An Audience with Tony Hayward, Chief Executive of BP," *The BP Magazine*, Issue 1, 2008.

Page 140 "Hayward has said . . ." Guy Chazan, "BP's Worsening Spill Crisis Undermines CEO's Reforms," *Wall Street Journal*, May 4, 2010.

Page 140 "He told one interviewer . . ." "An Audience with Tony Hayward, Chief Executive of BP," *The BP Magazine*, Issue 1, 2008.

Page 141 "Hayward gave a critique . . ." BP internal e-mail, Dec. 11, 2006.

Page 142 "Safety: There can be no . . ." BP internal communication, May 3, 2007.

Page 142 "In January, BP overtook . . ." Guy Chazan, "BP's Worsening Spill Crisis Undermines CEO's Reforms," *Wall Street Journal*, May 4, 2010.

Page 143 "The mantra in BP . . ." Ed Crooks, "BP: The Inside Story," *Financial Times Magazine,* July 2, 2010.

Page 143 "In Alaska, BP pleaded guilty . . ." BP Press Release, Oct. 25, 2007.

Page 143 "Hayward recognized that . . ." Ibid.

Page 144 "The panel's chairman . . ." Stanley Reed, Jessica Resnick-Ault, and Brian Swint, "BP Faces Extra Obstacles After Spill," *Bloomberg BusinessWeek*, May 31–June 6, 2010, 20.

Page 144 "The regulators continued . . ." BP Press Release, August 12, 2010.

Page 145 "After Inglis interrupted . . ." Ed Crooks, "BP: The Inside Story," *Financial Times Magazine*, July 2, 2010.

Page 147 "He repeatedly claimed . . ." Ibid.

Page 150 "A headline in the . . ." Helen Kennedy, "Tony Hayward: The Most Hated—and Most Clueless—Man in America," *New York Daily News*, June 2, 2010.

Page 152 "According to a transcript . . ." Joe Carroll, "BP's U.S. Future Teeters as CEO, Lawmakers Clash," Bloomberg News, June 18, 2010.

Page 152 "I think we can all conclude . . ." BBC website, June 20, 2010.

Page 153 "Hayward did not get . . ." Eduard Gismatullin and Brian Swint, "BP's Hayward Quits After Spill Shreds Pledge to Improve Safety," Bloomberg News, July 27, 2010.

Page 154 "I know what it is . . ." Ed Crooks, "BP: The Inside Story," *Financial Times Magazine*, July 2, 2010.

Chapter 9: Disaster on the Horizon

Page 156 "The blowout preventer . . ." Schlumberger oilfield glossary, Schlumberger.com.

Page 157 "When the weather cleared . . ." E-mail sent by BP Drilling Engineer Scherie Douglas to the Minerals Management Service on November 17, 2009.

Page 157 "The riser has a series . . ." "Drilling Basics," Diamond Offshore Drilling Inc., www.diamondoffshore.com.

Page 157 "Just a week after . . ." Alison Fitzgerald and Joe Carroll, "Cracks Show BP Was Battling Its Gulf Well as Early as February," Bloomberg News, June 17, 2010.

Page 158 "It was just passed around . . ." Transcript of hearings of Coast Guard Marine Board of Investigation.

Page 158 "BP's plan called for . . ." Ibid.

Page 158 "The last two times . . ." Joe Carroll and Laurel Calkins, "BP Pressured Rig Worker to Hurry Before Disaster, Father Says," Bloomberg News, May 27, 2010.

Page 159 "Well control is part . . ." Transcript of June 15, 2010 House Energy and Commerce Subcommittee on Energy and Environment hearing.

Page 160 "*Business Week* ran an article . . ." Steve Levine, "Exxon: Juggernaut or Dinousar?" *BusinessWeek*, February 5, 2009.

Page 162 "Frank Patton says he . . ." Mark Chediak, Joe Carroll, and David Wethe, "MMS Engineer Unaware BP Had to File Safety Document," Bloomberg News, May 11, 2010.

Page 165 "We would have used . . ." Transcript of House Energy and Commerce Committee hearing.

Page 172 "I wanted to do . . ." Copy of statement notes of Don Vidrine to the Coast Guard.

Page 172 "Vidrine called a well engineer . . ." Transcript of testimony of Chris Pleasant to the Coast Guard Marine Board of Investigation.

Chapter 10: BP Struggles to Survive

Page 178 "In the Asian culture . . ." Transcript of hearing of the House Energy and Commerce Committee, June 15, 2010, retrieved from http://energycommerce.house.gov/documents/20100615/transcript.06.15.2010.ee.pdf.

Page 181 "This is the only way . . ." Robert Reich, "Why Obama Should Put BP Under Temporary Receivership," *Huffington Post*, May 31, 2010, retrieved from www.huffingtonpost.com/robert-reich/why-obama-should -put-bp-u_b_595346.html.

Page 182 "Senate Majority Leader Harry Reid . . ." Reid video, retrieved from http://reid.senate.gov/newsroom/061410_bp.cfm.

Page 182 "As *Wall Street Journal* said . . ." "The BP Precedent," *Wall Street Journal*, Review & Outlook, June 18, 2010.

Page 184 "BP provided roughly 14 percent . . ." Brian Swint, "Obama Scolding BP on Dividend Favors Fisherman Over Retirees," Bloomberg News, June 10, 2010.

Page 184 "Neil Duncan-Jordan, of the National Pensioners Convention . . ." Louise Armistead and Myra Butterworth, "Barack Obama's Attacks on BP Hurting British Pensioners," *Daily Telegraph*, June 9, 2010.

Page 184 "Hall says gross negligence . . ." Margaret Cronin Fisk and Laurel Brubaker Calkins, "BP: Now Come the Fines," *BusinessWeek*, August 5, 2010.

Page 186 "While we realize we are suffering . . ." Testimony of Courtney Kemp, House Energy and Commerce Committee Hearing, June 7, 2010.

Page 186 "Hayward said on July 27 . . ." Stanley Reed, "Why Robert Dudley's BP Could Be Even Riskier," *Bloomberg BusinessWeek*, July 28, 2010.

Page 187 "Russians are "more philosophical . . ." Stanley Reed, "How BP Learned to Dance with the Russian Bear," *Bloomberg BusinessWeek*, September 23, 2010.

Page 188 "Browne gave Dudley's selection . . ." Ed Crooks and Catherine Belton, "Man in the News: Bob Dudley," *Financial Times*, July 30, 2010.

Page 189 "I hope five years . . ." Dudley, July 27 call with reporters.

Page 191 "BP has already been able . . ." Anousha Sakoui and Sylvia Pfeifer, "BP Raises $3.5 Billion in Bonds Sale," *Financial Times*, September 29, 2010.

Page 191 "These are the first . . ." "Dudley Sets Up New Safety and Risk Unit and Signals Sweeping Changes at BP," BP Press Release, September 29, 2010.

Page 191 "BP employees, he said . . ." Sylvia Pfeifer, "BP's New Chief Optimistic Over Resumption of Dividend Payment," *Financial Times*, October 1, 2010.

Page 193 "Roughly half of . . ." "The Role of Deepwater Production in Global Oil Supply," IHS CERA press release, June 30, 2010.

Epilogue

Page 195 "Later, he gave a talk . . ." Stanley Reed, "John Browne on the Future of Energy," *BusinessWeek.com*, November 23, 2007.

Page 196 "His message is both urgent and hopeful . . ." Browne, *Beyond Business*, 242.

Page 196 "At a book festival in Edinburgh . . ." Steven Brocklehurst, "Ex-BP Boss Lord Browne Did Not Discuss Lockerbie Bomber Release," BBC Scotland News website, August 15, 2010.

Page 197 "The oil spill might seem . . ." Edward Rothstein, "The Sea and the English who Tried to Master It," *New York Times*, August 18, 2010.

About the Authors

Stanley Reed is a reporter-at-large for Bloomberg News in London. Prior to joining Bloomberg News, he was London bureau chief of *BusinessWeek* magazine from 1996 to 2010. He has written extensively about the oil industry, the Organization of Petroleum Exporting Countries (OPEC), and the Middle East, as well as Britain and Scandinavia. Reed has covered BP for more than a decade. He accompanied John Browne on a trip to Russia in 2003. He has visited many oil projects, including BP's Thunder Horse platform in the Gulf of Mexico, Sakhalin II in the Russian Far East, Samotlor in West Siberia, and Champion West off Brunei. Prior to moving to London, he edited and often wrote *BusinessWeek*'s "International Outlook" political column. His work has also been published in *Foreign Affairs*, *Foreign Policy*, the *Nation*, and the *New York Times*.

A graduate of Yale University and Columbia Business School, Reed was a Knight-Bagehot Fellow at Columbia University Graduate School of Journalism from 1987 to 1988. He received the Best of

Knight–Bagehot award for 2003 for his coverage of the war in Iraq. Reed lives with his wife, Katherine, in Belsize Park in London.

Alison Fitzgerald, an award-winning investigative reporter at Bloomberg News, writes about the convergence of government and economics in Washington, D.C. Fitzgerald, a graduate of Georgetown University and Northwestern University's Medill School of Journalism, has been with Bloomberg News since 2000, covering the U.S. auto industry, the Federal Reserve, the U.S. Treasury, economics, and tax policy. Her coverage of the financial crisis and ensuing government bailout won her several awards, including the 2009 George Polk Award, and the "Best of the Best" from the Society of American Business Editors and Writers. Her work on the international food price crisis in 2008 won her the Overseas Press Club's Malcolm Forbes Award.

Fitzgerald started her career at the *Philadelphia Inquirer* as a reporter covering the New Jersey suburbs and criminal courts. She then moved to the *Palm Beach Post*, where she wrote about coastal development, migrant workers, and county government. She spent three years as a reporter and editor at the Associated Press, covering courts and government in Boston and working as editor on the international desk. Fitzgerald and her husband, Drew Kodjak, have three children and live in Takoma Park, Maryland.

Index

Index